JOHNNY MILLER'S
Golf for Juniors

Other books by Johnny Miller

Pure Golf, Doubleday, 1976

Other books by Desmond Tolhurst

Six Days to Better Golf, by Harry Obitz and Dick Farley, with Desmond Tolhurst, Harper & Row, 1977.

JOHNNY MILLER'S
Golf
for Juniors

Johnny Miller with Desmond Tolhurst

Illustrated by Dom Lupo

DOUBLEDAY & COMPANY, INC., GARDEN CITY, NEW YORK
1987

Library of Congress Cataloging-in-Publication Data
Miller, Johnny, 1947–
Johnny Miller's golf for juniors.

Summary: An instructional introduction to the game of
golf for first time and junior golfers.
1. Golf. [1. Golf]   I. Tolhurst, Desmond.   II. Lupo,
Dom, ill.   III. Title: Golf for juniors.
GV965.M468   1986   796.352′3   85-20630
ISBN 0-385-27943-4
ISBN 0-385-27944-2 (pbk.)

First Edition

Dedicated to my father

Contents

Preface

No one becomes a champion without help. I'm no exception. Looking back, I was blessed by our heavenly Father. He gave me the help of three fine people: my dad, John Geertsen and Karl Tucker.

From my earliest years, my father dedicated himself to my growth as a golfer. He even rearranged his work hours—working from midnight to 8 A.M. While I was in school he slept, so that he could be there for me in the afternoons. He always told me that I was going to be a champion—if I just worked hard. He instilled the work ethic into me, telling me that if I wanted to succeed, I had to work harder than anyone else was prepared to. If I made a good shot, he'd praise me; if I played a bad one, he never said anything. He literally gave up his time to work on my game, devising all sorts of creative ways to practice as well as getting me to countless junior tournaments. It was my father who put me firmly on the first rung of the ladder to success.

To John Geertsen, I also owe a tremendous debt. John never took a penny for the lessons he gave me. His labor of love gave me a firm grasp on the fundamentals of the game. He, too, always believed in me, and he always emphasized the positive. He's someone I turn to when I have a problem with my game.

Karl Tucker, my coach at Brigham Young University, also helped me immeasurably. He had a marvelous golf program at BYU. Through him, for example, I had the chance to go to Scotland, experience that later stood me in good stead in the British Open. He got me ready for the PGA Tour, but more than that, he helped me grow up.

In regard to the preparation of this book, I'd especially like to thank:

Chuck Brenkus, for his fine sequence and still photographs;

Dom Lupo, whose lucid illustrations of my ideas on the game are such a notable asset, and

Desmond Tolhurst, *Golf Magazine* contributing editor, who was always ready to "go the extra mile" in interviewing me and putting my thoughts into writing.

JOHNNY MILLER

JOHNNY MILLER'S
Golf for Juniors

1

The Perfect Start

If I had to start my career in golf all over again, I wouldn't change a thing. I had the perfect upbringing in the game. At five, my dad began my training by having me hit balls into a net in our basement. He taught me the basic fundamentals of the golf swing by checking my swing positions in a mirror. Then he took movies of my swing. He showed me pictures of the great players. He also made sure that I always had a goal to strive for.

Only after two years of this groundwork did he finally take me to the golf course. A little later, I began to take lessons from John Geertsen, then the professional at the San Francisco Club.

You should graduate to playing for score on the course only after you've built a pretty good swing. If you try to play for score before you can hit the ball reasonably well, you'll easily become discouraged.

There were and continue to be solid advantages to my father's methods. Hitting into a net frees you from worrying where the ball is going. Consequently you can concentrate on building your grip, setup, swing and hitting the ball solidly. These should be your first goals in golf.

The main problem with starting outside on a practice range is that you immediately become concerned with results. You see the ball slicing or hooking (curving in the air to the right or left) and try to steer the ball instead of working on your swing. Or you find it difficult to get the ball up in the air, and try to help it up. This often prevents you from swinging freely.

If you can, begin by hitting balls into a net. If you don't have a net or don't have space for one, then use a gymnasium or an indoor school. You'll find it really pays off.

Most indoor schools have large mirrors. A mirror allows you to work on your swing and actually see it as it is. You must know what your swing looks like even if it doesn't look as it should. You're much more open to suggestions if you can see that you need to improve in certain areas. No one can teach you if you think your swing resembles Sam Snead's and really your swing looks like Sam Shank's.

While a mirror is useful when working on your swing, the acid test of your progress is to make movies or videos of your swing when you are hitting a ball. Later in this book, I'll explain the seven key swing positions that you need to get right. A movie or video allows you to check these positions in your swing with those of the great players, or with sequence photos found in the multitude of books and magazines on golf.

From the beginning, you'll be trying to imitate certain positions or act on suggestions from your coach. What is key is to know whether what you *think* you're doing and what you're *actually* doing really match. If they don't, you'll be short-circuiting all over the place. Sparks will be flying and you'll make no progress.

If you don't have access to a video or movie camera, use a still camera. Just set it at its fastest shutter speed—preferably at 1/500 second or faster—and have someone snap away until you get the pictures you need.

In developing your swing, it's very natural and good for you to emulate the great golfers. In my own case, my dad provided me with the best books on golf available. When I was very young, I had a book by Sam Snead and another by Byron Nelson. In my mid-teens my dad picked up Ben Hogan's *Modern Fundamentals of Golf,* which is truly a great book and very advanced in its teaching.

Dad also had all the golf magazines. I remember one time looking at an article about Cary Middlecoff. Under one of the pictures, it said, "Middlecoff split the pin on this shot." I took this literally and thought that Middlecoff had split the pin the way Robin Hood split the arrow. I didn't know that it only meant to hit the ball right at the flagstick. Anyway, Cary became my hero and I copied his big deep knee bend through the ball.

I took my first professional golf lessons, from John Geertsen, when I was seven years old. When I was fifteen or so I met Tony Lema, then the assistant pro at the club, and I played a couple of rounds with him. I ended up imitating his out-to-in looping swing when I wanted to draw the ball.

When emulating the great golfers, it's important to know that no player has it all. Learn what each player does better than the others. It could be the swing, it could be iron play, short game or putting; whatever it is, apply the principles of what you learn to your game. In most cases, you will have to adapt them somewhat—after all, no two golfers are exactly alike.

Once you start playing the course, the best way to improve is, first, keep your score honestly. Don't take any Mulligans, putt out all those tricky two- and three-footers. Second, take your last ten rounds and average your score. It's no good thinking of breaking 80 if your average is 95.

To find the areas of your game you need to improve, make notes during your round between holes. Write down the number of fairways you hit. If you miss a fairway, note the side on which you missed it. Do the same with the fairway woods. Keep track of the irons you hit into the greens, the number of bunker shots, chips and putts.

Then analyze these notes. Say you notice that you had thirty-six putts, but also had six chips, in a round. Your chip shots might need work. If you hit a

1–5. My swing as a teenager, taken by my dad. The photos show that you can have a fine swing at any age—if you're prepared to work at it.

3

lot of greens, but your number of putts is high, it shows either that you're not hitting close enough with your irons or your putting is weak. You will know which it is.

My dad used to say to me, "Try to make your weakness your strength." I agree. If you can't hit a fairway wood, for example, practice with it until it becomes a favorite club. If you keep on practicing your weaknesses, you're going to be a strong player.

Another point my dad made was this: "If you want to be the best in your age group, you've got to be willing to work harder than anyone else. If all the others practice on the range for an hour and play eighteen holes of golf and then chip and putt for an hour, you've got to play more than that number of holes, and practice twice as hard."

That's the way it works in life. If you want more money in the bank, you have to put more money into your account. Talent will only get you to first base. To make it home, you must make a super effort!

Dedication is more important than ability.

It's not just physical effort that gets the job done. Hitting balls is not enough. I put in a tremendous amount of time practicing as a youngster, but I spent even more time thinking about the game as I practiced. I'm a great believer in putting this thinking into writing. Keep notes on your swing and the points you're working on. I have a pile of such notebooks at home, and I've found them very useful.

When I begin to have problems, I look over my notebooks. Say I have a problem with my swing, and I see an entry like: "Western Junior. Swing, working on a good shift to the left side and a high follow-through." This may be just what my swing needs. One thing is certain. Keys that worked for you once can often work again, *if* you can retrieve them. Again, it's money in the bank.

Whether you keep your notes in a notebook or a home computer, organize them under headings such as grip, address, swing, shot making, short game, and so on. The more easily you can retrieve the information you want, the more you will use it and the faster you will improve.

Another thing my dad instilled in me was the habit of always setting goals for myself. Whether you want to play the Tour one day or be a good amateur player, you must set an overall goal and then break it down into a series of steps.

Make these intermediate steps realistic, and move up the ladder one rung at a time. If you're a high 90s shooter now, then your short-term goal should be something like: "I want to shoot five strokes better by the end of the summer." But if you say, "By the end of the summer, I'll shoot in the 70s," you might be setting yourself an impossible task, and you'll ultimately be disappointed.

What you want is a series of small successes that eventually add up to one big success.

But remember: no pain, no gain.

In setting your goals, you must realize that improvement can come quickly from the 100s to 90, and almost as quickly from 90 to 85. However, from 80 to 75 goes much slower, and from 75 to 70 will seem like you're climbing Mount Everest. The ladder is steeper at the top, so have patience.

One more thought before we begin. Most books insist that there's only one way to swing. I don't believe that. To me, the swing falls into categories. If a certain type of swing has been successful on Tour during the past thirty years, then I won't say you should not swing that way. If you haven't seen it on the Tour, don't expect it to work.

I do believe that there are fundamentals you have to learn. I favor what could be called the simplest swing of all. Initially, I'll discuss that swing. However, I do want to show you the other types of swing. Then if you favor one of these swing variations, you'll understand what makes it tick and what you have to do to make it successful.

NOTE TO PARENTS

Teaching youngsters to play golf is a lot like building a house. You have to lay a solid foundation first. Your children should first learn the basics of the grip and stance even before they begin swinging. The next step is to acquire the basics of the swing before they set foot on the course.

The exact approach does vary, however, with the age your children start, and their degree of interest in the game.

If they begin when they are very little—say, two to four years old—just let them hit the ball and go chase it. It doesn't matter whether they hit it well or badly. Just let them have fun.

Don't worry if the child grips the club cross-handed. Of my six children, only Casi, my second girl, naturally gripped with the right hand below the left. The others all took hold of the club cross-handed.

A cross-handed grip helps small children control the club more easily. It doesn't feel as heavy to them. Also, the grip puts the left side in a very strong position, as it does in putting. It allows the child to develop left-side control of the swing. This is important.

The time to change them to a conventional grip is when they're five or six and have more hand and wrist strength.

As regards formal instruction, gear it to the individual child. My eldest son, John, Jr., now sixteen years old, had as great an interest in golf at age five as I did, and I was giving him pretty adult instruction at eight. My girls, Kelly (fourteen) and Casi (twelve), were never as serious.

What you must wait for is that golden moment when your youngsters are ready to become serious and learn the basics that will improve their game. In Kelly's case, this happened only a couple of years ago. She started asking me for lessons. A friend of hers in school was hitting golf balls and Kelly then began to think of it as a pretty neat thing to do.

It doesn't really matter what motivates children to learn golf. The thing to realize is that they must supply their own motivation, not yours. If you try to force the game down your children's throats, they will object, and you could turn them off the game for good. You should gently encourage and make golf available as much as possible.

Whether children should play left- or right-handed is really up to them and their particularities. A good case can be made for putting your strong side up front in the golf swing. Bobby Jones and Ben Hogan, two of the best strikers of a golf ball ever, were left-handed, playing with right-handed clubs. (Incidentally, so am I.) The left side is the leading side in the right-handed player's swing. Therefore, if you're left-handed and play with righty clubs, you have an advantage because your strong side is controlling the swing. Interestingly, Bob Charles, the fine New Zealand player, is right-handed, playing with left-handed clubs.

However, it's tough to be too dogmatic. Many right-handed people can't do anything with left-handed clubs, and vice versa. You should study what comes naturally to your children. If they naturally bat right- or left-handed in baseball, then that's probably the way they should hit a golf ball. Since baseball is a sport in which hitting left-handed is as well or even better accepted than hitting right-handed, it's a very good test. I do recommend playing right-handed because of better teaching and equipment.

Regarding equipment, if you have a very small child starting out, ask your pro shop whether they have some old clubs that they can cut down to fit your child. Most pros are very willing to do this; they realize your child is going to be both a customer and a pupil for many years to come.

You don't have to get a lot of clubs for a small child. A 5-iron and a putter are fine as starters. It's far more important that the clubs truly fit the child in length, size of grip and weight.

Watch out for getting the right size of grip. I've seen far too many youngsters with clubs the right length but with grips that are too thick. This forces them to hold the club like a baseball bat, thumbs around the shaft. I believe in children starting with the grip they'll use all their lives, whether that is an overlap or an interlock. Grips that are too large make that almost impossible, and your child will only have to change his style of grip later. If the pro doesn't have small enough rubber grips in stock, have him use ladies' grips, or order them, or ask him to get leather grips that you wind on by hand.

Usually, when you cut down a club, the weight is fine for most children. However, if your child is small and laboring with a club, take some weight out of the head, if possible. With a wood, you can take some lead out from under the sole plate. With irons, you can grind off the toe. Alternatively, cut off some of the toe using a hacksaw, or drill several holes partway through the back of the blade just above the sole.

One advantage of giving beginners only one club (other than a putter) is that they'll develop all sorts of shots with it: opening the blade and laying it back to get more height, closing it down to get more run. Seve Ballesteros learned to play with one club, a 3-iron, and today he is one of the great shot makers in golf.

As soon as your children get serious about the game, give them half sets. Don't bother with a driver—most children will only dribble the ball along the ground with so straight-faced a club. A good set is a 3- and 5-wood, 3-, 5-, 7- and 9-irons, pitching wedge, sand wedge and putter. That's all they'll need. Nine clubs, rather than fourteen, makes the bag lighter, incidentally.

Half sets also pick up where the single club left off. They force children to hit a particular club different distances. They'll become shot makers.

One last tip on equipment. If a child loves a club, don't get rid of it just because he's outgrown it. If I have one regret from my junior days it would be that I thought I needed a new set every two years or so. I junked more good clubs that way than I care to remember. Instead, merely lengthen the club or clubs about an inch a year.

My son John, Jr., had a 5-wood he loved from the time he was six years old. When he began outgrowing it, I just took the grip off, put a plug in the shaft and regripped it. I did this at least four times. Eventually, the club had a plug twelve inches long! After that, instead of putting a longer plug in it, I took off the grip, heated up the original shaft, and while it was hot, I took another shaft of the right diameter and just hit it into the original shaft. When it cooled, the two shafts were like one.

There comes a point, of course, when you should simply reshaft the club. But never throw away a good club. Clubs you love—especially woods, wedges and putters—are often impossible to replace. That's why you'll often see one or two "old favorites" in Tour pros' bags.

2

Be a Square

When I started golf, my father made sure that I had the correct grip. If your hands are in the right position, then it's much easier to hit the ball squarely.

The right grip is one in which the palms of both hands are square to the target. In other words, if you took your grip and then opened up both hands so the fingers were extended, the palms of both hands would be square, or at right angles to the target line (an imaginary line through the ball to the target).

The square grip is best, because your hands naturally return to a palms-facing-target position at impact. See this for yourself by standing up now and making a backhanded slap with your left hand at the side of a padded chair or sofa. Extend your fingers and slap the chair. No matter what the position of your hand when you started, the back of your left hand naturally will square up to the side of the chair at impact.

Now slap the chair with your right hand. Again your palm is square at impact.

Applying this to golf means that if you start at address with the clubface aimed squarely at the target, and your hands also are square, your hands return to this square position at impact. You'll hit the ball straight. With a square grip, it's as though your grip and the clubface were one unit.

The square grip is also called the neutral grip, because it's midway between two other grips: the strong grip and the weak grip.

In the strong grip, the palms are tilted to the right (for a right-handed player). If your clubface is square to the target at address, and you use a strong grip, the squaring-up action of the hands tends to close the clubface at impact. The usual result is a hook, the ball curving in the air to the left. The only way to keep the clubface square at impact is by forcing the palms to stay tilted to the right. It can be done, but it's not the most recommended or widely used way among top players.

In the weak grip, the palms are tilted to the left. At impact, the hands tend to turn to the right, opening the clubface. An open clubface normally produces a slice, or ball curving to the right. To square the clubface at impact,

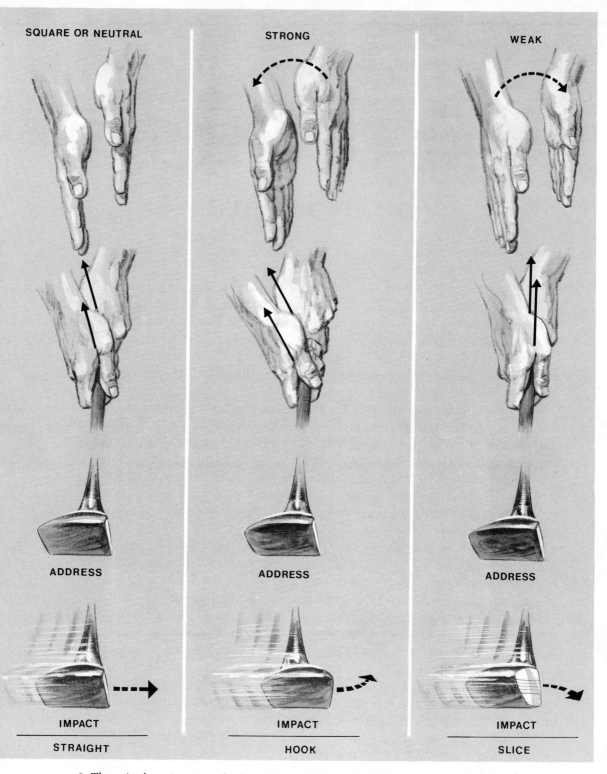

SQUARE OR NEUTRAL	STRONG	WEAK
ADDRESS	ADDRESS	ADDRESS
IMPACT	IMPACT	IMPACT
STRAIGHT	HOOK	SLICE

6. The grip that gives you the best chance of hitting the ball straight is the square, or neutral, grip, in which the palms of both hands are square to the target line. This is because the palms always tend to return to a square position at impact. In this grip, the V's of both hands point up at your right ear. If you take a strong grip, with both palms tilted to the right and the V's pointing up at the right shoulder, the hands tend to twist to the left at impact, closing the blade and causing a hook. If you take a weak grip, with both palms tilted to the left and the V's pointing up at your chin, the hands tend to twist to the right at impact, opening the blade and causing a slice.

you have to force your hands to the left. Again, it can be done, but it's not easy. This grip requires strong hands and much more effort to be effective.

In short, if you start either with a weak or a strong grip, you have to make compensations during your swing in order to hit the ball straight. With the square, or neutral, grip, you don't have to make any compensations. It eliminates many potential problems.

THE OVERLAP, INTERLOCK AND TEN-FINGER GRIPS

Most of the players of the PGA Tour use the overlap, or Vardon, grip, in which the little finger of the right hand fits in the groove between the index finger and the middle finger of the left hand. I have used this grip from the beginning. Jack Nicklaus, Tom Kite and Bruce Lietzke, among others, use the interlock grip, the little finger of the right hand lying between the index and second fingers of the left hand, so that the fingers interlock.

A lot of people will tell you that, if you have short fingers in relation to the length of your palm, then you should use the interlock, or that longer fingers make the overlap more desirable. However, I don't believe either of these rules. I've seen too many exceptions to them.

Choosing between overlap and interlock grips is like deciding between chocolate and strawberry ice cream. Both grips bring the hands close together so that they work as a unit. Your hand and wrist action is the same with either grip. So try both of them, then choose the grip that's most comfortable and works best for you. Choose the one that will coordinate your hands to work as a unit.

One other grip deserves mention: the ten-finger grip. Here the hands are put on the club with no overlap or interlock.

At one time practically every teacher used to start children with the ten-finger grip. Even today many teachers still do it, claiming that a child's hands aren't strong enough to use the interlock or the overlap grip.

I don't agree 100 percent with this thinking. First, with the ten-finger grip, there's too much risk of the hands working independently during the swing. Second, when you get older and stronger, the same teachers would tell you to switch to either the overlap or the interlock.

Changing your grip is very difficult at any age. So why not start with the grip you will use all your life? There have only been a few good pros using a ten-finger grip.

THE LEFT-HAND POSITION

In positioning the left hand, support the club with your right hand holding the bottom of the grip. Put your left hand in the "slapping" position and press

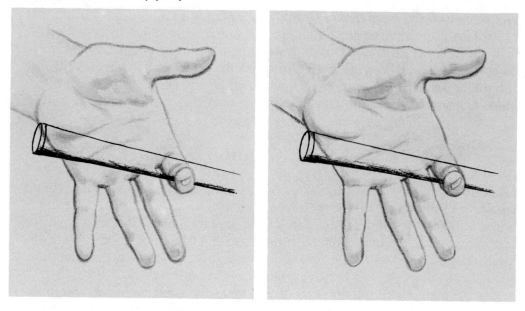

7. Although every good golfer places the grip in the middle joint of the left index finger, the position of the grip across the left hand can vary. The most versatile position is the one in which the grip lies between the base and the middle of the muscle pad at the heel of the hand. 8. If you like to use maximum hand action, as I do, you may prefer to hold the club a little more in the fingers, the grip lying at the base of the pad. 9. Golfers who use very little hand action often prefer to put the grip higher in the hand, on top of the pad. 10. Avoid this position, in which the grip lies on the Lifeline, for full shots. The fingers can loosen, and you lose control. You can use this position in putting.

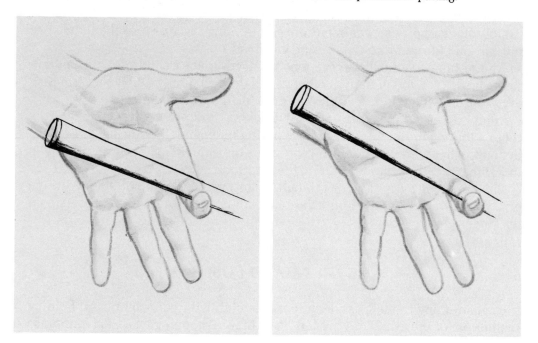

the palm lightly against the left side of the grip. Then curl the index finger and place the grip in the middle joint of the finger. The grip should run across the palm so that it lies between the base and the middle of the muscle pad at the heel of the hand. Now close the fingers around the grip and lower the muscle pad and thumb to the grip so that the thumb points straight down the club shaft.

If you do this correctly, your left thumb should be slightly to the right of center on the grip. If the top of the grip is 12 o'clock, your thumb is about 1 o'clock. Another checkpoint. The V formed by the index finger and thumb of your left hand should point up at your right ear.

If you find that your left thumb is in the 12 o'clock position and the V points up at your chin, then you've accidentally taken a weak grip; you tilted the palm a little to the left while taking your grip. Similarly, if you find that your left thumb is in the 2 o'clock position and the V points at your right shoulder, you've taken a strong grip.

In both cases, take the grip again, paying particular attention to keeping your palm in the square position until the grip is complete.

One question that youngsters always ask me is this: How tightly should I grip the club? You obviously don't want to hold the club so loosely that you can't control it, or so tightly that your muscles stiffen. It's impossible to put the right amount of pressure in words, but here's an easy way to find it.

Take some practice swings with just your left hand holding the club. You'll quickly find the pressure that gives you control without stiffness.

Not every good golfer positions the club in the left hand as I've described. They all place the grip in the middle joint of the index finger, but the angle at which they set the grip across the hand varies.

I told you that the grip should lie between the base and the middle of the pad at the heel of the hand. This position allows you to use a lot of hand and wrist action or very little, as you prefer. It's the most versatile.

However, players who like to use maximum hand and wrist action, position the grip lower in the hand, more in the fingers. I'm a good example of this. I grip the club at the base of the pad. This sets the club in a slightly flatter position (club shaft closer to horizontal) than when you hold it between the base and the middle of the pad. Fuzzy Zoeller does much the same thing. With this grip, you can generate tremendous club speed.

At the other end of the scale is a golfer like Jim Simons, who uses very little hand and wrist action. Such a golfer often prefers to position the grip higher in the hand, on top of the pad. In fact, the grip runs diagonally across both hands. This sets the club in a slightly more upright position (club shaft closer to vertical). At address, such golfers position their hands in an almost straight line from the left shoulder to the ball (as seen from the player's left). This grip makes your swing simpler, but it also slows your club-head speed through the ball. You're going to be very accurate but not long. Don't consider this grip until you feel you're strong enough to hit the ball like an adult.

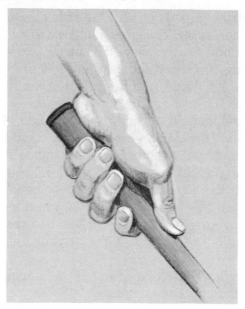

11. However you position the club in the left hand, for full shots you need to have some of the pad on top of the grip. Then you can hold the club securely between the pad and the back two fingers of the hand.

Above all else, avoid placing the club so much in the middle of the hand that it lies on the Lifeline, between the base of the thumb and the pad. Some players like to use this grip for putting, but only duffers use it in the full swing. With the Lifeline grip, only the fingers hold the club. There's no support from the pad. During the swing, you can't pin the grip handle against the pad for support. The fingers can loosen and you lose control of the club, especially at the top of the backswing.

You must have some of the pad on top of the grip so that you can hold it securely between the pad and the back two fingers of the left hand. You can't play good golf with the club wobbling about in your left hand.

THE RIGHT-HAND POSITION

Unlike the left-hand grip, which is a palm-and-finger grip, the grip in the right hand always should be in the fingers.

Having positioned your left hand correctly, bring the right hand to the right side of the grip in the "slapping" position. Curl the middle two fingers and rest the grip in the bottom joints of the fingers. Then overlap with the right little finger, or interlock. Finally, lower the palm so that the groove of the palm fits snugly on top of the left thumb, close the index finger around the club and lower the thumb to the left side of the shaft.

Correctly done, the V's of both hands now point up to your right ear. Again, if the V of your right hand points at your chin, then your grip is too weak. If the V points at your right shoulder, it's too strong. Both the V's should be the same.

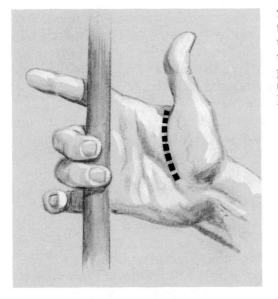

12. The grip in the right hand is always in the fingers. To find the right position, curl the middle two fingers and place the grip in the bottom joints of the fingers. In the completed grip, the groove of the right palm (broken line) should fit snugly on top of the left thumb.

Don't try to check your grip at address, because your head is to the right of the grip and you'll get a distorted view. Instead, bring the club up to waist level, the club shaft about horizontal and centered in the middle of the body, with the toe straight up. Then you'll get the right picture.

If you have problems getting the right hand in the correct position, then pay more attention to how you fit the right palm on the left thumb. The Lifeline of the right hand should be on top of the left thumb, and the fleshy muscle at the base of the right thumb should be on the left side of the left thumb. If you work on getting a really snug fit, you'll get it right.

With my own grip, I like to separate the right index finger slightly from the other fingers of the right hand. If this feels comfortable to you, do the same. It gives more support and power at impact. If you prefer to keep the fingers together, that's okay too, but almost all good players have this gap.

The overall pressure in the right hand should be a little less than in the left at address, but you should feel a lot of pressure in the downswing against the knuckle of the right index finger, especially in the hitting zone. This is very important. If you release the club correctly, you will feel the same amount of knuckle pressure from a point halfway in the downswing to a point halfway in the follow-through. If you release too early, the pressure is gone.

THE SQUARE GRIP VERSUS OTHERS

Time after time, I see young players come out on Tour with strong grips. After a few years, many change to a weaker grip, a grip very close to the square, or neutral, grip I've recommended to you.

Bruce Lietzke, for example, had a strong grip when he first came out, but now he has pretty much a V's-to-the-right-ear grip. Mark McCumber has done the same thing. In the future, Hal Sutton will be the one to watch. He's now using a strong grip, but I predict he'll go to a square grip before too long.

Why do they change? Because the pressure on Tour exposes any weaknesses in technique. As amateurs, these players may have been able to get away with a strong grip. They came to realize, though, when the heat's on, they can get a big hook which puts them in trouble and loses tournaments. You also have poor distance control. It's like having a snake in your bag—you never know when the hook is going to strike.

I want to take this opportunity to address this because so many youngsters, my own included, tend to use a strong grip if left to themselves.

The strong grip may feel powerful, but this powerful feel is really an illusion. The strong grip makes you close the blade on the backswing. Then, on the downswing, you have to make a big lateral move with the legs, rather like Lee Trevino, and hang on to the club tightly so that the clubface doesn't close. The ball flies extremely low unless you cup your left wrist and scoop the ball. The worst feature of the strong grip is that you never release the grip properly. You're fighting the natural rotation of the arms and hands to the left through the hitting area. Children need this rotation to get as much power as they can. That's why I'll never understand how some teachers still teach children a strong grip—they're dead wrong, in my opinion.

Do any players on Tour use the weak grip, V's at the chin? The answer is yes. The reason why a pro will use a weak grip is that he wants no part of a hook—it not only flies violently to the left, it also runs a long way on landing. A hook can put you in a lot of trouble. So these players prefer to use a grip that, if anything, will give them a fade, a ball that flies straight and falls to the right. A fade sits down quickly; it's a shot you can control.

I personally use a weak grip, and as a result, I'm extremely accurate with the middle and short irons. I'll explain the reasons for this later. However, I must admit that, with the driver, my weak grip has almost shown up as a fault—I had to make a big effort to square up the clubface at impact.

After all my years on Tour, I'm switching to a neutral grip, with the driver down to the 3-iron, but I'm retaining my weak grip on the middle and short irons. The results have been terrific.

In the future, I believe that many of you are going to use a neutral grip in the long game and a weak grip in the middle and short game. We'll get into this in depth later on.

3

The Address

The complete position you assume just before starting the swing is called the "address." Taking your address is like aiming a gun. If your sights are lined up at the target, you'll have a good chance to hit the bull's-eye when you squeeze the trigger. But if your aim is off, you'll miss unless you correct the fault during your swing—a risky business.

In fact, once you've developed a pretty good swing, you'll find that, when your game goes sour, the first thing you should check is your address.

I remember one time at the Doral tournament, in Florida, I was leaving most of my shots to the right. I tried every swing change imaginable to cure the problem. Then I discovered that I simply hadn't been aiming the clubface properly. It was open—aimed to the right of the target. Once I aimed the clubface squarely at the target, I again hit the ball straight.

AIMING AND ALIGNMENT

Aiming a wood club squarely at the target is fairly simple. Sit the club on the ground and square the top line of the clubface with the target line. With irons, square the leading, or *bottom,* edge of the blade with the target line. *This is important.* I see a lot of youngsters aiming with the top edge of an iron. Then the blade is shut—aimed to the left of the target.

It's worth noting that you must square the clubface before taking your grip. Then you position the left thumb exactly at 1 o'clock every time. If you take your grip with the club soled on the ground, it's easy to square the clubface before gripping. However, if you prefer to take the grip with the club up in front of you at waist level, do it with the toe of the club pointing straight up. That guarantees the clubface is square before you grip.

When you start in golf, I recommend you take what is called a "square" stance, in which imaginary lines across your toes, knees, hips and shoulders are parallel to the target line. It's as though the clubhead and ball were on one railroad track and your feet were on the other. The clubhead/ball track

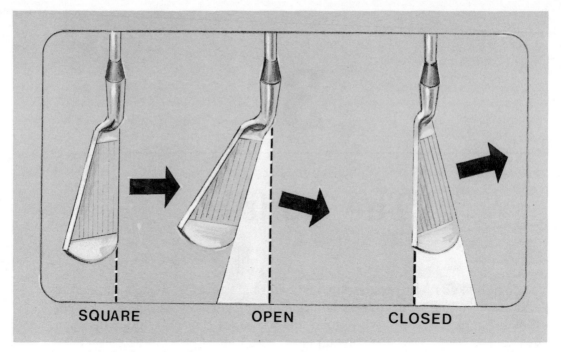

SQUARE   OPEN   CLOSED

13. If the leading edge of an iron is square to the target line, the clubface is square. If the leading edge is aimed right of target, the clubface is open; if left, it is closed. Don't make the mistake of aiming with the top edge—you'll close the clubface.

14. In a square stance, imaginary lines across your toes, knees, hips and shoulders are parallel to the target line. 15. In an open stance, the lines point to the left of square. 16. In a closed stance, the lines point to the right of square.

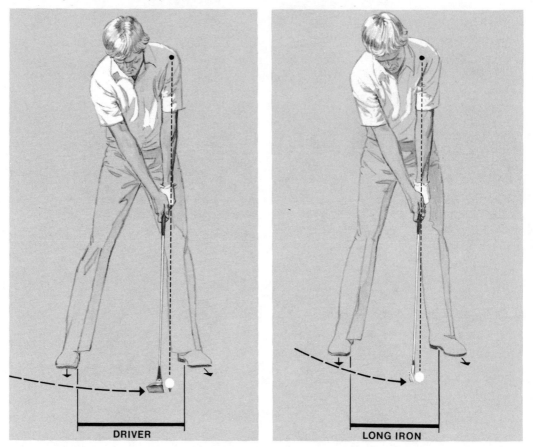

17–20. *Across.* With the driver, you need a sweeping arc. So you play the ball about off the left heel and adopt a wide stance to put your weight behind the ball. As you go down to the shorter, more lofted clubs, you narrow the stance and play the ball farther back. This puts your weight more over the ball, to give you a more descending blow.

extends all the way to your target. The foot/body track runs parallel to the target line extending to a point just left of the target.

You also should understand what is meant by an "open" and a "closed" stance. In an open stance, your feet, knees, hips and shoulders are aligned to the left of square, and in a closed stance to the right of square.

Open and closed stances are used for special shots which I'll describe later. Even on these shots, you usually aim the clubface at the target.

FOOT AND BALL POSITION

In the '60s and early '70s, everyone, including Jack Nicklaus, was saying that you should play all normal shots, from the driver down to the sand

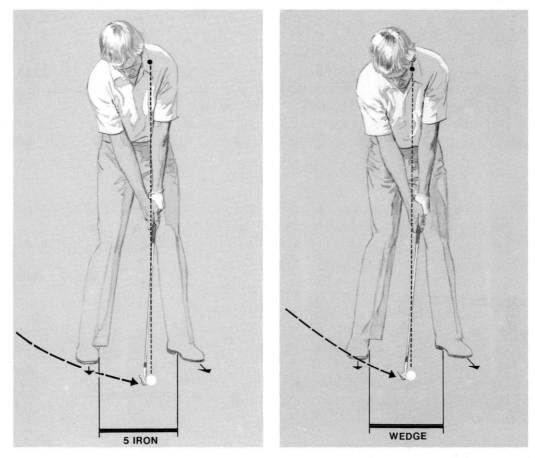

wedge, off the left heel. It was claimed that this made things simple. To create the proper width of stance for a particular club, all you had to do was move your right foot. For a driver, you placed the right foot just outside your right shoulder. This put your head and weight behind the ball and produced the sweeping arc needed. Then you gradually narrowed your stance by spreading your right foot less far as you went to the fairway woods, long irons, medium irons and short irons. Gradually, on the shorter irons you became more centered over the ball, with the narrower stance creating an ever steeper downswing arc.

Although I agree basically that you create the proper width of stance and weight distribution with the distance you spread your right foot to the right, it's not the whole story. I've found that you can't play the ball in one position and be totally effective. So has Jack Nicklaus.

At the time Nicklaus was playing everything off the left heel, he could never hit a short iron well. Now, with a driver he plays the ball off the inside of his left heel, and with a wedge he positions the ball just a little ahead of the center of the stance. What's good enough for Jack Nicklaus should be good enough for the rest of us.

Although all golfers tend to talk of ball position in relation to the left heel, the best way to get correct ball position is also to relate it to the left shoulder. The socket of your left shoulder is the fulcrum of your swing. So, on a driver, you want the ball opposite the left shoulder socket. On a wedge, you want the ball opposite the left side of your neck. As you go from the driver to the wedge, you keep notching the ball back from the shoulder socket, so that you hit down on the ball more and more. Take an iron, and try making a practice swing with your eyes closed, taking a divot. You'll see the divot hole is more in the middle of the stance, rather than on the left heel.

Another way of getting the right weight distribution is to be aware of where your head is. On a driver, your whole head will be about six inches behind the ball. On a normal wedge, it will be just behind the ball, with the ball lined up on the left side of your neck.

Using your left heel and your head as guides is probably easier while practicing or playing. However, I do recommend you frequently check your left shoulder position with key clubs in a mirror.

The way you set your feet is also important, because it affects the way your body moves during the swing. As a starting point, place your right foot at right angles, or square, to the target line. The right leg then can resist the turn of the upper body in the backswing. You create a lot of tension in the right leg, like winding up a rubber band, so that it thrusts automatically to the left in the downswing.

In contrast, you don't want much tension in the left leg on the backswing. So turn the left foot slightly outward so that the left side can move freely and clear to the left in the downswing and follow-through.

Before I leave the subject of ball and foot position, it's worth adding that the type of grip you use does affect ball position. With a strong grip, the big lateral leg drive in the downswing puts the bottom of your arc farther forward, so you'll need to put the ball about an inch farther forward in your stance than I've recommended. With a weak grip, you should play it about an inch farther back, because the club comes up sooner in the follow-through.

SPRING LIKE A TIGER

When I set up to a ball, I try to get the feeling that I'm a tiger, about to pounce on my prey. Sometimes I feel as though I could jump up ten feet in the air.

To get the feel of this, stand with your feet about shoulder width apart, your arms hanging down at your sides. Now pretend you're going to jump straight up. Without thinking about it, you'll find that: your weight is 50–50 on each foot, with the weight on the ball and heel of each foot; your knees are slightly flexed; your upper body is bent slightly forward at the waist, your back straight; your rear end definitely is out to counterbalance the weight of the upper body, and your head is up. The whole position is alive and springy.

Besides having the weight balanced between the balls and heels of the feet, also put a little weight on the insides of the feet. Do this by turning the knees slightly toward each other. This gives you a more solid stance and helps the legs work properly during the swing. Setting the left knee inward encourages the left leg to work behind the ball on the backswing. Setting the right knee inward braces the muscles of the right leg. You can then turn the upper body, going back around what feels like a solid, pretty much fixed, right leg. It also discourages swaying to the right.

I'm often asked the question: "How far should I stand from the ball?" The answer is simple. Correct posture and the length of the club dictate the distance. Here's how:

Take a driver, then stand erect, the insides of the feet shoulder width apart. Take your grip with the club out in front of you at waist height, both arms extended. Get into the "tiger" position, bent at the waist, butt out, knees flexed and slightly inward. Then let the clubhead fall slowly to the ground, taking your arms and the upper body with it. That's the correct posture and distance from the ball for that club. If you repeat this procedure with a short iron, you'll find that you have to lean forward just a little more from the waist to allow the club to fall to the ground. That is correct.

THE FINISHING TOUCHES

Although the "tiger" image and drill I've just described will put you in a pretty good position over the ball with every club, there are a few additional points you should know.

Chin Up. When you did the club-dropping drill, you probably found that, especially with a wood, you were forced to look at the ball out of the bottom of your eyes. That is correct. This is because your head was erect on your spine when you started and retained the same position relative to the spine as you leaned forward. Again, correct. You'll very seldom see a good player looking at the ball out of the center of his eyes except on a putt or maybe a chip shot. If you allow your chin to slump onto your chest with full shots, which is what you have to do to look at the ball out of the middle of your eyes, the chin blocks the shoulders from turning properly in the backswing. So, keep your chin up.

High-Low. If we could hold the club with both hands at the same level on the grip, it would make golf a lot easier. Automatically the shoulders would be level and square, and the arms would hang down square with the target line.

However, because the right hand is below the left on the club, the only way to set up with the left arm extended and the shoulders square is to *lower* the right shoulder a little. This gives you leverage. Be careful; if you aren't, the right shoulder can get pushed forward so that the shoulders are open. This is one reason why so many golfers slice.

A good way to prevent this ever happening to you is to occasionally practice setting up to the ball with only the left hand holding the club. Leave your left shoulder where it is, but drop your right shoulder down enough so you can comfortably touch your right knee with your right hand. This puts your shoulders in correct position. Now complete your grip.

Elbow Position. The position you adopt with your elbows is largely a result of how you grip. To understand this, take a very strong grip, both V's outside your right shoulder. You'll see that the left elbow faces the target and moves away from your body. At the same time, your right elbow tucks down close to your body. From this position, you tend to swing the club very much to the inside. You take it away low, flat and around the body.

Now set up with a superweak grip, the V's between your left cheek and left shoulder. The left elbow now turns and moves close to the body. The right arm straightens and pushes the right shoulder forward so that the shoulders are very open. This produces an upright swing.

If you take the neutral, or square, grip I've recommended to you, the V's at the right ear, the left elbow is in a comfortable position between the two extremes. The right elbow is slightly bent. The left elbow points at the left hip, the right elbow at the right hip. A line through both elbows is parallel to the target line. You may find that your right elbow has a tendency to straighten a little, as with the weak grip. If so, work on it looking in a mirror until the shoulders and elbows are parallel.

Wrist Angles. If you were going to punch somebody, you would use a straight anatomical position of the left wrist, not a cupped one. Make a fist with your left hand and make believe that you're going to throw a punch. Then extend the fingers of the hand, and you see that the fingers are dead in line with the forearm. Then make the fist again and note the slight angle at the left wrist formed by the back of the left hand and forearm. That's the position you want in golf, as in boxing.

When you address the ball, set your hands so that the top of the handle is on top of the ball. This slight forward tilt of the shaft allows you to set up with the straight position of the left wrist. It also encourages the whole left side to lead during the golf swing. With your hands *behind* the ball, you have a tendency to sweep the club too much, and you have to make a big weight shift to get back to the ball. With the hands too far *ahead* of the ball, the opposite happens. You hang back on the right side in the downswing.

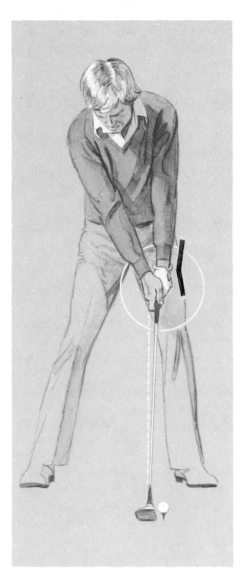

21. When you address the ball, set your hands so that the top of the handle is directly above the ball. This slight forward tilt of the shaft allows you to set up with the left wrist in a straight anatomical position.

22. At address, your wrists should be slightly arched. To do this, your hands should be between one and one and a half hand widths away from your body.

Another angle you should study is the position of your wrists from the side (as another person would see it if he were standing to your right, looking down toward the target). If you take your address aiming away from a mirror and then look back into the mirror, you can see that your wrists are slightly arched. You need this slight arch so that your hands and arms work in one piece away from the ball.

You should have the same amount of arch in the wrists no matter where you position the grip in the left hand: between the base and the middle of the pad at the heel of the hand, at the base of the pad or on the top of the pad.

The one thing you must avoid is getting the wrists overarched. This usually comes from adopting a left-hand grip with the club across the top of the pad. However, you can get into this position even with the left-hand grip I've recommended.

A good rule of thumb is to have your hands between a hand width and a hand and a half away from the body. I don't ever recommend two hand widths unless you're using the "palms" grip (grip on top of the pad). Then you're probably going to be overarched and be forced to play with a dead-handed swing, one with very little hand and wrist action. As I said earlier, strong adult players can play with a dead-handed action. They can muscle the ball out far enough, even without much hand and wrist action. But a youngster can't, so don't try.

To ingrain the fundamentals of the grip and address, let me stress again the importance of working in front of a mirror. Check and recheck the points I've made so far. They are and will become, as you will see, the basis for your whole game.

4

Pattern Your Swing

If you have ever watched Tour pros play a few holes, you have probably noticed that each one of them has his own set pattern of taking address. From the time he takes the club from his bag to the moment he starts his swing, he goes through the same series of steps in the same order.

This "pattern," or "routine," as it is sometimes called, is essential to good golf. It gives you the time to prepare physically and mentally for the shot. It creates confidence, because you build a good address step by step. It also keeps your mind on what you want to do with the shot. If your mind is filled with images of the swing you want to make, the way you want the ball to fly and where you want it to finish, it has no room for negative thoughts.

I no longer think of my pattern when I play. It became automatic a long time ago. But when you're starting out in the game, you want to establish a set pattern as soon as possible. To help you, here's mine as a guide.

1. I start from a position behind the ball, looking down at the target. Holding the club loosely in my left hand, I fix the target line in my mind.
2. With my eyes on the target line, I move diagonally left, to a point at right angles to the target line through the ball, and turn, facing the ball.
3. I now take my grip, step toward the ball with my right foot leading and take a little half swing.
4. I place the clubhead behind the ball square to the target line.
5. I put my feet together.
6. I spread my left foot to the left—the exact distance depending on where I want to position the ball.
7. I then spread my right foot to the right to give me the right width of stance for the club I'm using.
8. From this point on, I move my weight from one foot to the other, back and forth, by slightly lifting each foot. I waggle the club three or four times as I look at the target.
9. Just before I swing, I flex my right knee inward a little, shifting the weight slightly to the left side. As the weight shifts back to my right side, I'm off into my backswing.

23. A good address pattern breeds confidence and consistency. Start from a position behind the ball. Fix the target line in your mind and pick out a spot on it to which you'll align the clubface and your body. You can use a spot about a yard in front of the ball or one out about twenty yards.

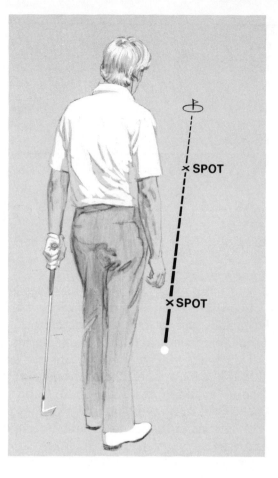

Here are some additional points you need to know.

You start from a position behind the ball to get a true picture of the target line. As you step to the side and set up to the ball, you need a way of keeping track of the target line, because that is your guide for setting up with the clubface and body square.

There are two basic ways of doing this. The first is called "spot alignment." Pick a spot in front of the ball on the target line, and then set up square to the line from the ball to the spot. The spot can be anything distinctive, such as a speck of discolored grass, a bare spot of ground and so on.

Whether you pick out a spot a short distance in front of the ball—say within a yard—or a longer spot, say twenty yards in front of the ball, depends on whichever suits you best. Personally I find it impossible to use the short spot, because when I set up to the ball, the spot appears to me to be left of the target line (even though I know it's on the target line). Other people, I know, have similar optical illusions. However, if I use a spot about twenty yards in front of the ball, it looks as though it's on the target line. On the other hand, Jack Nicklaus uses the short spot all the time and very successfully.

The second method involves running your eyes back and forth between the ball and the target as you set up. In other words, you set up to the whole

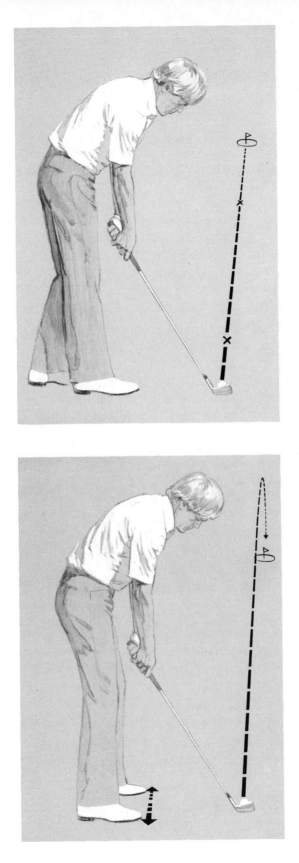

24. Move diagonally to a point at right angles to the target line, take your grip and step toward the ball with the right foot, setting the clubface square to the spot. 25. Put your feet together, the ball centered between them. Be very aware of the target line or your spot. This enables you to make the next move correctly. 26. Spread your left foot to the left and the right foot to the right to the correct stance width, your toes on a line parallel to the target line. From there, keep moving, shifting your weight slightly from one foot to the other. Make a waggle as you visualize the shot, then go immediately into your backswing.

length of the target line. Jim Colbert is a winner on Tour who uses this technique.

I should mention that if you spot-align, use it only in setting up. Once your feet and body are positioned square, forget about the spot and start running your eyes from the ball to the target. This helps you program the swing and shot you want to make, and feel the distance you want to hit the ball.

One thing I do in my pattern that a lot of players do is put my feet together before spreading them apart. I find this helps me position the ball correctly as well as spread my feet so that stance and body are square.

Another popular method is to step into the ball with the right foot leading. Then spread the feet without putting them together. For me, this makes proper ball position and body alignment too much a matter of chance. However, if you can consistently set up in a good position this way, it's not wrong. Arnold Palmer, for one, does it this way.

Whichever way you do it, here's an additional tip on getting the right ball position. Once I've set the clubhead squarely behind the ball, I draw an imaginary line with my eyes from the front edge of the club right to where my left foot is. I use the line to help me spread my left foot the right distance.

You may have noticed that there's no practice swing in my pattern. The purpose of a practice swing is to rehearse the swing you're about to make, and also to relieve any tension in the hands and wrists. However, you do risk making a poor practice swing, and then repeating that poor swing at the ball. That's why today the closest I get to a practice swing is a little "waist-high to waist-high" movement. That relieves any tension. As for rehearsing the swing, I do this in my mind. Don't waste your energy on a full practice swing.

If you make a practice swing, do it well away from the ball. I learned this the hard way at the age of eight. I was playing in my first big tournament, the Northern California Junior. I hit a good drive off the first tee, then made a practice swing before my second shot too close to the ball—and hit it on the toe of the club.

Once you've set up to the ball, the worst thing you can do is stand still. This lets tension creep in. Instead, keep in motion, moving your weight slightly from one foot to the other, and waggling the club.

Regarding the waggle, this can be a little back-and-forth movement of the club made with the wrists, it can be a complete wrist break, it can be any movement that keeps the club in motion as you look at the target. My own action, for example, is a lifting and dropping of the club. I've seen golfers making little circles with the club, and so on. No matter what waggles you use, try to keep them to a maximum of four. If you do any more than four, you run the risk of becoming tense again.

The last move in any good pattern is a forward press, a motion that leads directly into the backswing. If you watch good players, you'll notice that they don't start the swing from a dead stop. Instead, they make a small motion forward, toward the target. The action starts in the right knee. The knee kicks inward a little, shifting the weight momentarily to the left foot. Then the right knee flexes back, shifting the weight to the right foot, and the backswing starts.

The forward press is a "must." When you've completed your address, you're basically balanced evenly on both feet (50-50). If you tried to start the swing from there, you'd feel very awkward. To make a *good backswing,* you need to shift about 80 percent of the weight smoothly to the right foot. The "forward-back" move with the right knee is the easiest way to do it, because you're already shifting the weight as you begin.

An important point about the forward press is not to overdo it. I've seen some youngsters make a forward press of the right knee and the handle of the club several inches or so. That's far too much, because such a big movement forward throws the whole address position out of kilter and leads to a faulty swing. A little nudge forward of the right knee and club, of, say, an inch or two, is quite enough.

Once you've established your own pattern, don't vary it. The whole idea of the pattern is to make you more methodical and therefore more consistent. You can't be consistent if you take two waggles on one shot and four on the next.

Finally, if something disturbs you in the middle of the pattern, stop and start again from the beginning. After a while you'll find that you go from the first step in the pattern to the last in one unbroken flow. Once the flow is broken, it disturbs your concentration to try to pick up the pattern in the middle. It's far better to start over.

5

The Swing

An auto mechanic has to have a thorough knowledge of an engine before he can take it apart for repair and put it back together again. In the same way, you should have a good overall idea of what makes the golf swing tick before you make a start tinkering with it.

While a car engine has many parts, the golf swing has only four: 1. wrist action; 2. arm action; 3. body turn and 4. weight shift.

There are two chief movements in the golf swing, each combining two of the four parts:

1. The Sledgehammer movement. The wrists and arms together create an up-and-down movement very similar to a blacksmith striking downward on an anvil.
2. The Scythe movement. The body turn and weight shift combine to make a movement very similar to a man cutting grass with an old-fashioned scythe.

To see how these movements blend together to create the total golf swing, first address a ball with a 7-iron, as I've described previously. Imagine that instead of having a golf club in your hands, you have a sledgehammer. You're going to beat down on top of the golf ball, squashing it flat on the ground.

Raise the 7-iron straight up over your right shoulder just as if it were a sledgehammer, and your wrists and arms will have worked in the same manner as they would in a good golf swing. Now keeping the arms and club in the same position in relation to the right shoulder, turn your shoulders 90 degrees to the right, letting your arms and club turn with your shoulders. Also, allow your hips to turn to the right with the shoulders so that 70 percent of the weight shifts to the right foot. The left knee will come forward and to the right, and the left heel will rise slightly off the ground as much as needed. You're now in a pretty good top-of-the-swing position.

Now return to the address position, unwinding the shoulders and then lowering the club.

Raise the club again straight up in front of you like a blacksmith, only this

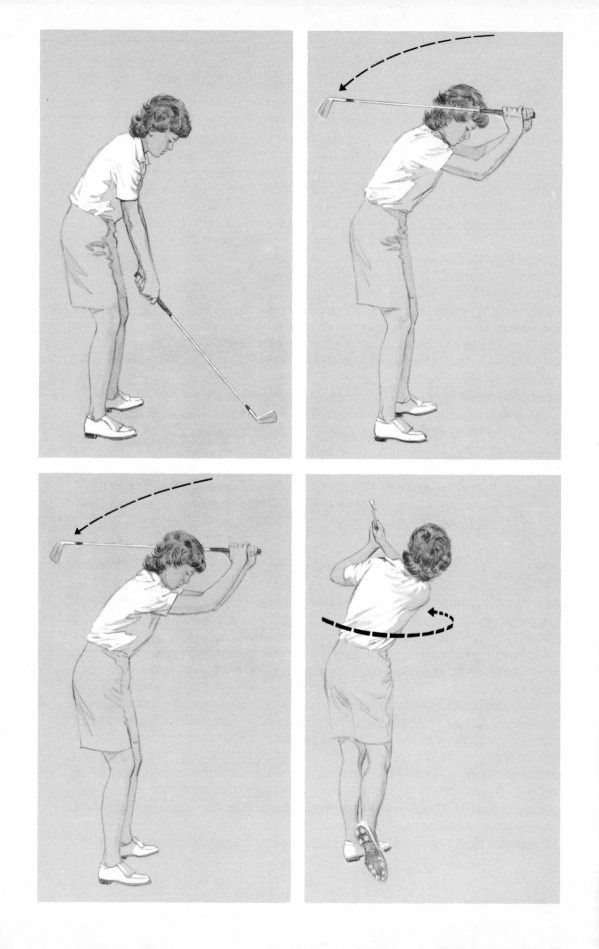

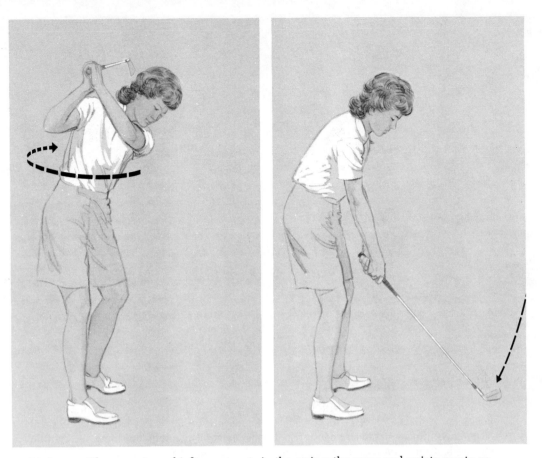

27. *Across.* There are two chief movements in the swing: the arms and wrists create an up-and-down, "sledgehammer" movement, and the body turns and the weight shifts like someone using an old-fashioned scythe. You can see how these movements blend to form the golf swing in the following exercise: Take your address position. 27a. Raise the club over your right shoulder as though using a sledgehammer. 28. Turn your shoulders 90 degrees to the right. You're now in a pretty good top-of-swing position. 29. Return to address. 30. Raise the club over your left shoulder. 31. Turn the body 90 degrees to the left. You're now in a pretty good follow-through position.

time over your left shoulder. Then turn your shoulders 90 degrees to the left, allowing your arms and the club and your hips to turn along with the shoulders, so that your weight shifts 100 percent to your left foot and your right heel is pulled from the ground. You're now in a pretty good finish position.

THE HALF SWING

While the "Sledgehammer/Scythe" exercise gives you a good idea of how the complete swing works, I don't want you to start on the full swing immediately. As you've seen, in the full swing the club goes up behind you on the

32. Start learning the swing with the half swing. Here I show my son John, Jr., the key positions. Address. 33. Top of swing; the hands are about waist height. 34. Impact. 35. Follow-through; hands are again about waist height. Note: John has hung back a little on his right foot—imitate my body position on this one.

backswing and then goes up and behind you again in the follow-through. When you're beginning the game, you're probably going to lose control of the club at some point and develop some bad habits.

Instead, I want you to start hitting balls with the half swing that Ben Hogan used. With a shorter swing, the club stays in front of you and you'll be able to check yourself every step of the way.

If I were with you on the practice tee, I would walk you through the whole action first. Let's try that. Again, use the 7-iron.

1. **Address.** Set up with a square grip, a slightly open stance, your feet a little less than shoulder width apart and your hands over the ball. Put 60 percent of your weight on your left foot, 40 percent on your right.
2. **Top of Swing.** Take your club back in slow motion to the point where your hands are at about waist height. Stop and check that your shoulders are turned about half as much as for the full swing, that your left arm is slightly bent or comfortably straight but not stiff, that your right arm is folded 90 degrees into your side and that your wrists have bent

upward (or cocked, as it is called). There should be more weight on your right foot (70 percent) than your left (30 percent), and your left knee should be bent to the right and forward about opposite the ball. The toe of your club should point directly upward.

If you have any difficulty with this, you can break the motion down into two actions, as in the "Sledgehammer/Scythe" exercise. Start from the address. Bend your wrists straight upward and raise the hands to waist height. Then make a half turn to the right before checking your arms and weight shift.

3. **Postimpact.** Now slowly swing through until the club is about one foot past the ball. Stop. This is the *only* point in the swing where *both* arms are *straight* at the same time! *The right arm folds* on the backswing, as we've seen, and from this point on into the follow-through, the *left arm folds.* Check that your shoulders have returned to square, parallel to the target line, and that the club shaft points up at the middle of the chest. Other points to check: 90 percent of the weight is on the left foot, but your chin is still in back of the ball, as it was at address. Your right foot should have rolled to the left onto its inside edge, with your right heel just starting to come up from the ground.

4. **Finish.** Swing slowly through until your hands are at waist height. Your shoulders will have made a half turn through. Your left arm will have folded 90 degrees, while your right is comfortably straight. You'll be standing fairly erect, with 100 percent of your weight on your left foot,

your right knee kicked inward to the left and your right heel off the ground. Your wrists will have bent upward (recocked), and the toe of your club will be pointing straight up.

Now that you've identified the key swing positions, take some slow swings, starting from the address, going back to the top and swinging through to the finish. Once the whole action feels pretty smooth, put a ball down on a good lie (or on a low tee if your practice ground is worn), and hit it with the half swing. Continue hitting balls in this fashion.

Before I go on to the full swing, let me try to anticipate some of the difficulties that may come up at this point.

1. **Wrists are stiff.** If you notice that your wrists aren't cocking and uncocking as they should, chances are that your grip is too tight. A tight grip stiffens your wrists. Hold the club lightly enough so that you can feel the weight of the club swing back and through.

2. **Elbows don't fold.** If you find that your right elbow doesn't fold readily going back or the left elbow, going through, do a few practice half swings baseball-style. Stand erect and swing the club around you at about waist level. Going back, make sure the clubface opens—at the top, the clubface should be face *up;* swinging through, the clubface closes; in the finish, the clubface should face *down.* You'll find that such practice swings almost force you to fold each elbow correctly. Then return to the regular half swing.

3. **Slicing.** If the ball is curving to the right, check your follow-through. Probably, the clubface is pointing upward. This means that at impact the clubface was open, imparting slice (left-to-right spin) to the ball. The reason for this is that you're not rotating your left forearm and hand in the downswing. At the top of the swing, the toe of the club should point straight up, and in the finish the toe should again point up. Execute this action in slow motion and study how your left arm rotates the shaft in an anticlockwise direction.

   To overcome the slice, take your regular address, then take your right hand off the club, letting it hang at your side. Note that your left thumb is pointing down the shaft at the ball. Now swing the club slowly to the top of the half swing, and note that the left thumb is now pointing directly to your right, and the toe of the club is up. Swing slowly back to impact—your left thumb should again point at the ball. Then swing slowly through to the waist-height finish position and note that your left thumb points at the hole, and the toe of the club is up again.

   When you slice the ball, your thumb at the finish points backward, almost to where the ball was on the ground, and the *clubface* is up. There's no rotation. Do this one time so you can feel it. Then develop the correct feel of the action in your left thumb, and make certain you do it every time.

4. **No rhythm, no click.** If your swing lacks rhythm, or you fail to hit the ball solidly, you're probably trying to overcontrol the action; you're not letting it happen. If so, think of brushing the top of the grass for the first few inches of the backswing; then, on the downswing, think of brushing the grass for a few inches in front of the ball. You'll soon develop a solid swinging action back and through.

When you've hit one ball, don't rake another one over quickly and hit again. Always hold your follow-through for a few seconds, and watch the ball land and finish rolling. If it was a good shot, ingrain the feel of it in your mind—it will help you program future shots.

If it was a poor shot, try to figure out what you didn't do right, before hitting another shot. Also, before every shot, start from behind the ball, pick out a target and go through your whole preswing routine. It's when you leave out some or all of your routine that you get to hitting balls too quickly, too mindlessly—and learn nothing.

For the chronic "rusher," here's another good tip. Instead of emptying out the practice-ball basket in front of you, which encourages the quick "rake-over and hit" habit, tip the balls out to the right of and behind you. Now you have to move your feet to get another ball. Then you won't be tempted to skimp on your routine.

As you continue hitting balls, you'll find that the full swing "grows" from this half swing without your thinking about it. Just by swinging back a little faster and swinging through with a little more power, you'll automatically swing back a little farther and through a little farther. That's fine, and just what you should expect.

THE FULL SWING

Once you've worked up to a full swing with a 7-iron, you're ready to work on the full swing with all your clubs. As with the half swing, you have to get key positions correct first before you can expect the full swing to be correct. The value of working on key positions is this: If you can perfect the key positions—and there are only seven of them—then all the positions in between the key positions will be correct too.

The key positions are as follows: 1. address; 2. halfway back; 3. top of swing; 4. halfway down; 5. impact; 6. postimpact, and 7. follow-through. Basically, you should work on them in the following ways.

1. **Slow motion and stop.** Starting from the first key position, address, for example, you would swing slowly back to the second position, halfway back, and stop. Then you'd check the second position, and correct it where necessary. Then you should hold the position for about ten sec-

36, 37. John, Jr., demonstrates how the full swing "grows" from the half swing without your thinking about it. Just by swinging a little faster, you'll automatically swing back and through a little farther.

onds, before swinging in slow motion to the third position, the top of the swing, and so on.

Although you can work on the key positions outside, checking them yourself, or having a buddy check you out, one of the best ways to do it is indoors, in front of a full-length mirror. Then you can compare yourself to the pictures in this book and know you're right.

I also believe in working on the positions with a heavy club. Initially, get a weighted doughnut and put it on the end of your club. Later, as you reach your full strength, you could use a heavy practice driver. Both should be available through your pro shop.

Using the heavy club has two major benefits: It's a very good form of exercise, since the golf swing uses both sides of the body. It also ingrains the key positions faster than if you used an unweighted club. In short, it's exercise you're happy to do, because it improves your golf swing.

Do be careful, however, where you practice your key positions. Once, when I was fifteen and playing in the Northern California Junior, I was in the dining room and had a club in my hand. I saw a mirror and, without thinking, I swung back to check my top-of-swing position. I hit a chandelier with the clubhead, and a big chunk of it fell and cut a vein in my hand. Blood squirted up to the ceiling! Even worse, though, I couldn't play in the tournament, which really upset me. Make certain you won't hit somebody or something *before* you swing a club. All of my six children have had their heads opened up by clubs.

2. **Drills and swing keys.** Drills are ways of practicing the whole swing or parts of the swing. By perfecting a motion, you improve a key position or positions. Swing keys are simply mental images that help you swing better. I'll be using both to help you when we discuss the key positions in detail.

3. **Photos, movies and videos.** Although I've mentioned this before, I'll repeat that you need pictures of yourself hitting shots. Check your key positions against the illustrations shown in this chapter, and then you'll know how you're progressing and what you need to work on.

THE SEVEN KEY POSITIONS

Before I begin on the seven positions of the swing, it's worth pointing out that they're not something you practice when you're just beginning and then don't have to bother with any more. I still work on them, and I know a lot of other Tour players do as well. They're as important for you at sixty years of age as they are at six. You never get too good or too old to review these basic fundamentals over and over.

Position One: Address.

Since we've discussed all the components of the address earlier, I'll just summarize the main points: club aimed at the hole; feet, hips and shoulders square to the target line; right foot square, left foot turned a little to the left; ball lined up on the inside of the left foot for driver, progressively farther back in stance with shorter clubs; right foot outside right shoulder with driver, progressively closer to the left foot with shorter clubs; "tiger" posture; weight evenly distributed between balls and heels of feet (50–50), weight set slightly on insides of feet; chin up, left shoulder slightly higher than right, left arm nicely extended, right arm slightly bent, elbows parallel to target line; "square" grip, hands over the ball; "straight" left wrist, wrists slightly arched.

Slow Motion to Position Two

From the address position, make a forward press. Kick your right knee to the left a little, feel the weight move to the left foot (60–40 percent). Then flex your right knee backward to the original address position to start the swing. Rock forward 10 percent, then rock back.

The takeaway should feel like a "one-piece" motion of the whole body dominated by left-side action; your hands and arms, your shoulders, your legs, should all start moving together.

As the weight shifts to the middle of your right foot, roll your left foot inward, with your left knee breaking toward the ball and to the right. Your right leg retains its flex, and its muscles firm up as the hips turn as though in a barrel. After the "rock back," your hips don't move any farther to the right. Important to note is that, with longer clubs, the "rock back" is a bigger move, because your right foot is placed farther to the right.

Meanwhile, you start to turn your shoulders, taking the "Y" formed by your arms and the club back with the turn. Your right arm begins to pull back and fold just as if you were going to throw a ball. The "pull back" action of your right arm makes your left arm stretch and extend. This in turn sets up a leverage action that starts cocking the wrists.

Position Two: Halfway Back

Stop and hold Position Two, and check that: your weight is mostly on the inside of your right foot, with some weight still on the inside of the ball of your left foot; your hips are turned a little, your shoulders turned about 45 degrees.

Your left shoulder is and should be behind the ball. It has moved several inches from the address position. Your left arm is extended, your right arm folding. At this point, there should be about a 90 degree bend in your right arm. If your right arm folds too much (the angle in your right arm is less than 90 degrees), it causes your left arm to bend too much. If your right elbow is at 90 degrees, your left arm stays extended. Your wrists are slightly cocked, the club shaft horizontal and parallel to the target line, and the toe of the club is pointing straight upward. Your left wrist is still in the square position.

Slow Motion to Position Three

Continue the motions begun in the takeaway. Shift more weight to the middle of your right foot, as the left knee moves to the right and the heel lifts. The hips and shoulders turn, with the head moving a little more behind the ball. Your shoulders carry your arms and the club back with your right arm folding more into the side. Your wrists should continue cocking.

Position Three: Top of Swing

Now stop and hold Position Three. Be sure to check that your right knee is directly above your right foot, with 80 percent of your weight on your right foot. Your right foot should be flat. If your right knee and your weight remain on the inside of your right foot, you have a lot of control, but that is not a full swing. If your right knee goes too far to the right, so that your weight is on the outside edge of your right foot, then you've swayed; you lose the coil in your right leg. Your hips should be turned as fully as possible without letting your right knee move farther right than the "right knee over right foot" position; your left knee is bent behind the ball, and your left heel is rolled up off the ground—less if you're super flexible, more if you're not flexible; your shoulders are turned to their maximum, with your left shoulder behind the ball; your hands and the club are above your right shoulder; there's tension in your left latissimus dorsi and deltoid muscles; your left arm is extended, and your right arm folded into the side at a 90 degree angle; your left wrist is in the straight position and your wrists are fully cocked, with your right wrist hinged back in the "waiter's tray" position; the club shaft is about horizontal or a little beyond horizontal and parallel to the target line.

Essentially, you'll feel as though you've planted your right foot and leg firmly and then turned your whole left side around and against it. You're "behind" the ball and ready to swing through it.

Slow Motion to Position Four

Start the downswing by smoothly planting your left heel. Make your weight shift to the left by driving your right knee left. At about the same time, your left knee should begin bowing to the left. The action of your knees turns your hips to the left, and they in turn unwind your upper body. I'd like to describe this leg action in a bit more detail. It's often described as a lateral motion to the left up against the left hip, then a turning motion to the left. Actually, the two movements—sliding and turning—occur simultaneously. The action is best described as a slide/turn—a slide with a turn incorporated in it.

As your knees make their move, try to keep your shoulders passive. This allows your arms and the club to "drop" down to hip height. In other words, you don't alter the angle between your hands and the club or unhinge your right elbow until your hands reach hip level. The motion should feel as though your arms, hands and club are dropping down as though by gravity. It's as if you were swinging a weight on the end of a string in a semicircle. The first move the weight makes as it changes direction is due to gravity.

Up to this point, I've described the backswing as one movement and the downswing as another movement with the top of the swing separating the two. During an actual swing, the downswing starts before the backswing ends. When hitting a ball, your right foot and right knee start their move to the left just before your hands and the club reach their farthest point back. In this way, backswing and downswing blend into one continuous movement.

Position Four: Halfway Down

Stop and hold Position Four. Check that your weight is balanced on your left foot and the inside of your right foot; both knees are still flexed, with your right knee kicking in to the left; your hips are about square to the target line; your shoulders are still a little turned to the right compared to the address position; your left arm is extended, right elbow bent and in to the side; your left wrist is in the straight position, and your wrists are still cocked; and the club shaft is pointing straight down at the target line. Your head is in the same position as it was at the top of your swing. Your weight at this position is 50–50.

Slow Motion to Position Five

Nudge your right knee to the left, turning your hips a little to the left and bringing your shoulders square to the target line. Move most of your weight to your left foot. Your right foot rolls farther to the left, and your heel may rise a little. Rotate your arms anticlockwise as you start releasing the angles in your right arm and wrists. Keep your head back.

Position Five: Impact

Stop and hold Position Five. Check that 80 percent of your weight is on your left foot, with your right foot rolled onto its inside edge, right heel up a little, right knee kicked in; your hips are turned up 45 degrees to the left of square, shoulders are square to the target line; your left arm is extended;

your right arm is still a little bent; your hands are slightly ahead of the ball, your left wrist in the "straight" position (if you're using a weak grip, your left wrist should be slightly bowed, your left wrist leading the back of your left hand); the clubface is square to the target; your right wrist is 90 percent uncocked; your head is approximately in the same place as it was at address.

You start your swing with your hands opposite the inside of your left thigh. However, if you study pictures of top players at impact, you'll see that the hands and the club shaft are centered on the crotch. This position gives them maximum power. The amount of lateral movement is determined by how big a lead of the hands a player makes. If he has a strong grip and makes a big lead of the hands to keep the clubface square, he has to make a correspondingly larger lateral movement to center the shaft at impact. A player like myself, with a weak grip, makes less lateral movement.

Slow Motion to Position Six

Nudge your right knee to the left just a little more, turning your hips and shoulders a little more to the left, taking your arms, your hands and the club to a position just past your left leg. Release the angles in your right arm and wrist.

Position Six: Postimpact (About one foot past impact)

Stop and hold Position Six. Check that your hips and shoulders are turned to the left fractionally more than at impact, both arms are fully extended and your left wrist is in the straight position. Your head should still be back in impact position.

Slow Motion to Position Seven

Your right knee should continue to drive to the left, turning your hips to the left. Your whole body should rotate to the left and gradually move to an erect position. Allow your head to release and come up with your body. Your left arm folds at the elbow as your arms swing upward, the right forearm rotating over the left. About halfway into the follow-through, your left arm should be bent 90 degrees. Similarly to the backswing, you shouldn't let your left arm collapse. Your weight should continue to shift to your left foot, another 10 percent more than impact.

Position Seven: Follow-through

Stop and check that you are in a balanced position, with your weight on your left foot, on the outside edge of your left heel; only the tip of your right

38. POSITION ONE: Address

39. POSITION TWO: Halfway back

43. POSITION SIX: Postimpact

42. POSITION FIVE: Impact

40. POSITION THREE: Top of swing

41. POSITION FOUR: Halfway down

44. POSITION SEVEN: Follow-through

foot is on the ground; your right knee is in front of and close to your left knee; your left knee retains its flex; your body is erect, your hips and shoulders facing left of target, your belly button pointing left of target, the cheeks of your rear end tight together; your head is up, looking at the hole; your hands are above your left shoulder; your wrists have recocked, your left elbow is 90 degrees bent, no more; your club is behind your back. Your left wrist should still be in the straight position.

THE IMPORTANCE OF WEIGHT SHIFT

I've recently been working with a swing computer called the "Sport Tech Golf Swing Analyzer." It costs over $10,000, but it is an unbelievable machine. Among the information it yields is your weight distribution at address, halfway into the backswing and at impact. This is how I have been able to give you percentages of where your weight should be at these points in the swing. I'd like to expand on this here.

The figures I gave you in the previous section (on the "Seven Key Positions") were those you should use for normal shots in the long game, using the driver, fairway woods and the 1-, 2- and 3-irons. With these clubs, set up at address with 50 percent of your weight on each foot (50–50). At the top of your swing, your weight should be 80 percent on your right foot, 20 percent on your left. At impact, 80 percent of your weight should be on your left foot, 20 percent on your right foot.

However, with the middle irons (4-, 5- and 6-irons) and the short irons (7-, 8-, 9-irons and wedges), the percentages are a little different. At address, put 60 percent of your weight on your left foot, 40 percent on your right. At the top, your weight should be 70 percent on your right foot, 30 percent left. What this means is that you are keeping your weight a little more on the inside of your right foot, in contrast to the long game, in which you shift your weight to the flat of your right foot. At impact, you have 90 to 100 percent of your weight on your left foot, 0 to 10 percent on your right.

These different weight distributions at address are created by taking the correct width of stance, which I described in Chapter 3. The correct weight shifts help you produce the more "sweeping" blow you want in the long game and the slightly descending blow desired in the middle and short games.

The percentages are approximations, because we're all a little different. Some pros shift 90 percent, or even 95 percent, of their weight onto their right foot at the top in the long game and have 90 or 95 percent of their weight on their left feet at impact. What is important to note is that there is a weight shift to the right foot going back, and to the left going through.

The type of grip naturally affects the weight shift on the downswing. Pros with strong grips—Lee Trevino, for example—are almost 100 percent on the left foot at impact. The stronger your grip, the more weight you shift laterally in the downswing. The weaker your grip, the more you tend to hang back on your right foot.

This factor was very important to me, with my weak grip. When I first got on the machine, I was only 60 percent on my left foot at impact. Now I'm up to 80 percent left, 20 percent right, exactly matching my shift of 80 percent right, 20 percent left at the top (long-game figures).

The machine has really helped me. I've seen such an improvement in my own game as well as my son John, Jr.'s, game, and other people's, too. Besides the weight factors, the machine also tells you how fast your backswing is; your clubhead speed at impact; whether your swing plane is correct; whether your clubface is open, closed or square at impact; your angle of attack on the ball—steep, shallow or in between—and how far the ball went.

The machine doesn't tell you your weight shift on the forward press. However, I would guesstimate it at 10 percent. I would also say that you should have about 10 percent more weight on the left foot in the follow-through than at impact.

If you have a chance to get on one of these machines—at a Tour tournament, for example—do so. You'll learn a lot.

DRILLS AND EXERCISES

I've dealt with two of the more important drills already: the "Sledge-hammer/Scythe" drill, which explains the components of the swing, and the "left thumb" drill, which teaches the rotation of the left arm through impact. Here are some other favorites of mine.

1. **One-handed swings.** For the right-handed person, there's nothing better for developing the muscles of the left forearm, wrist and hand than hitting balls with only the left hand holding the club. As a start, just hit the balls with a 9-iron or a wedge using a half swing. Later, when you get stronger, you can graduate to what I practice. I can hit a 7-iron about 145 yards with just my left hand, and my 4-wood about 200 yards.

   "Left-hand only" swings also teach you that a gradual cocking of the wrists during the backswing is a natural action. If you try some "right hand only" swings, you'll also find yourself cocking your wrists from the start of your swing.

2. **Swinging a weighted club.** Probably the best exercise for the golf swing is the golf swing itself using a weighted club. This develops all the muscles you need and, more important, *only* the muscles you need. Besides the "swing and stop" method I've just described, you can make full swings back and through. When making full swings, swing slowly at first—you want to build up your golf muscles, not tear them.

Another way to use a heavy club is to start at the top of your swing. Hold this for about thirty seconds, and then swing through. You can check your top-of-swing position, then start down. (You can also hit balls this way with a regular club—it's a terrific drill.) You'll soon find that the method I've described—starting down with the knees—is the most efficient and generates the most clubhead speed.

The best swings, to me, when I watch them in slow motion, make the golfers look as though they are swinging something very heavy. Jack Nicklaus is a perfect example of this. He never flips at the ball with his hands; he just drives the whole club—from handle to clubhead—right through the ball. The heavy club helps you develop such a swing.

3. **Rough stuff.** One thing I used to do when I was young was to hit a lot of balls out of high rough. I'd take a wedge and just plow through it. It's a tremendous exercise for developing your hands, wrists and forearms. It also makes you use your whole body to hit the ball. A great image for a strong hit is to imagine that you're going to hit something that's very heavy. Hitting through rough really helps you feel this strong impact, stressing the shaft and compressing the ball.

4. **Step through.** A lot of beginners get a good backswing, shifting their weight nicely to their right foot, but when they make their downswing, they hang back too much on their back foot. They often end up in what is known as a "Reverse C" position, their backs very much curved away from the target. You should try to avoid this at all costs. As you get older, you can really hurt your lower back with this action. A very good drill is to take a 7-iron, swing back, and then, as you swing through the ball, allow your right foot to step over your left. Even on a driver swing, you should be able to lift your right foot off the ground when you're in the follow-through position. These two drills help you finish in the correct, erect position, as well as help you drive your whole body through the ball.

5. **General exercises.** I've studied physical conditioning a lot over the years. In golf the extensor muscles—the ones that straighten your arms (as opposed to the flexors, the muscles that bend your arms)—are very important. Yet most of us in daily life don't use our extensors much, if at all. It's practically all flexors. To build your extensors, do pushups this special way: Do the down movement quickly (that's flexors), but emphasize a strong, slow movement coming up (extensors). Also, don't hold the down position very long. For your hands, squeeze grips are very good, and curls, with barbells, for the forearms. Anything you do for your lower body is terrific: cycling, running and so on. Short sprints are best—in golf you need bursts of power, not prolonged power. Don't forget the jump rope—you can use it indoors or out.

SWING KEYS

One of the most important things to realize about golf is that the body works from mental images—pictures. Of course, when you are just beginning the game, you won't have a clear mental image of the swing, because you've probably never seen it before. You simply have to start by emulating the swings of the great players. As you progress, you'll find that swing keys, mental images that help you swing better, become more and more useful to you.

Swing keys come in two forms: part-swing keys and whole-swing keys. Part-swing keys, applying to only a part of the swing, are most useful when you're working on one thing that is giving you trouble. Here are some examples of part-swing key applications:

- You're gripping too tightly: imagine you're holding a little bird in your hands at address, rather than a club.
- Your arms are too tense at address: imagine your arms are like ropes hanging down or are made of cooked spaghetti.
- Your back is bent over too much: imagine you're a soldier at attention, and stand proud and tall.
- You're not getting the right knee flex: imagine you're a tiger springing on his prey.
- You're picking up the club too quickly in the takeaway, and your shoulders and legs are lagging behind: imagine the club is a super heavy broom and you're "sweeping" the club away in "one piece."
- You're rushing the change of direction of the swing: think "pause at the top."
- You're starting down with the upper body: think, "Drive the knees."
- You're releasing the angles in your right arm and wrist too soon: think, "Drop and rotate"; that is, drop your arms and club from the top, then rotate the club from toe up to toe up through impact.
- You're flicking at the ball with your hands: think, "Drive the handle [of the club] past the left knee."
- You're not hitting solidly: imagine at address that there's a wall running from your left shoulder to the ball, at right angles to the target line. Try to return both of your hands and the clubface square to the wall at impact.

Whole-swing keys are particularly useful when you need some help out on the course. Out there, you shouldn't be thinking of parts of the swing. You have to find something to key the whole movement when things go wrong.

A good whole-swing key is "Swing the whole club, not the clubhead." There's a great tendency in all golfers to have the clubhead going at one hundred miles an hour through impact, but the handle end going five miles per hour or even backing up, away from the target. If you swing both ends of the club in the same direction at all times, you won't have that problem long. If you're getting frozen over the ball and are not shifting your weight from side to side, then think, "Right foot, left foot": plant your weight on your right foot going back and your left foot in the forward swing. If you're not getting the proper turn of the body going back and through, then think, "Right hip, right shoulder back; right hip, right shoulder through."

One of the most important overall considerations in the swing is tempo. I used to think that a very slow, deliberate takeaway was the best. I don't believe that any more. It's all too easy to go back slowly, then snatch the club down quickly from the top of the swing in a frantic attempt to get enough clubhead speed through the ball. I think you're far better off swinging the club back at a reasonably upbeat pace—but not so fast, of course, that you derail the swing—then slowing down gradually as you near the top of the swing and almost pause at the top. On the downswing, start slowly, then gradually and smoothly accelerate through the ball with maximum speed at impact—just like the backswing but in reverse. Correct tempo is much like the action of a clock pendulum.

I think every golfer has to find his own personal "red line" in regard to swing tempo. In other words, relating swing speed to the revolutions per minute (RPM) of an auto engine. Let's assume your swing has a red line of 7,000 RPM, producing a clubhead speed of 115 mph at impact. Here's how varying your RPM affects your results.

7,500 RPM: This produces approximately 116 mph clubhead speed at impact. It's the maximum effort you can make. However, you're over your red line. You're swinging so hard, you're out of control. You have bad balance and you "blow" your engine for certain.

The results are the occasional "gorilla" shot, the maximum distance you're capable of, but a tremendous number of mishits. You are and will remain very inconsistent.

7,000 RPM: This produces a little less clubhead speed at impact, approximately 115 mph. This is your "red line." You're swinging very, very hard and you have mediocre balance. A speed of 7,000 RPM will probably work on an occasional shot—say once or twice in a round. I use it, for example, where I need an extralong drive or on a long fairway wood shot on a par-5 hole where there isn't a lot of trouble. I never swing at my "red line" with my irons.

The results are maximum distance, but still some mishits, and inconsistency.

6,500 RPM: This produces approximately 113 mph clubhead speed at impact. This is the RPM you want to use on practically all full shots. It's definitely the tempo you should use on your long irons. You're swinging smoothly, have good balance, and hit the ball solidly.

The results are maximum performance, very, very little loss of power, consistent hits. You might not hit your longest "gorilla" shot at 6,500 RPM, but your average "mean" shot is longest and straightest.

6,000 RPM: This produces approximately 110 mph clubhead speed at impact. You're swinging more easily than at 6,500 RPM. This tempo is good for middle and short irons.

The results are a slight loss of power but a lot of control.

The first time I ever really studied RPM with Tour players was at the first Long Drive contest in Atlanta. I was expecting these pros to get up on the tee and swing "out of their shoes" at the 7,500 RPM or even at 7,000 RPM. The fact was they all swung very close to their comfort zone, between 6,500 and 7,000 RPM. They really seemed to be using their normal tournament swing, trying to get a solid hit. Interestingly, Nicklaus says he never tries to swing harder. When he wants more distance, he just makes a bigger turn going back.

On the average, 6,500 RPM is what you want. This is the speed Lee Trevino and Gil Morgan swing at. To find this optimum swing speed, go out to the practice tee and, when you've warmed up, hit several balls as hard as you can. That's 7,500 RPM. Then throttle back very gradually on successive shots until you're losing a little distance. That will be approximately 6,000 RPM. Then gradually increase the speed of your tempo again. The point where you most consistently get your long hits is 6,500 RPM. You're swinging hard but hitting the ball solidly and finishing in good balance.

Training yourself to swing at lower speeds than your 6,500 RPM mark is very important in shot making, as we'll see later.

The best way to use swing keys is not during the swing itself. Rather, imagine yourself executing the key as you picture the swing before stepping into the ball. Alternatively, make a practice swing using the key. On no account try to hit the ball thinking of the key; you'll most likely mess up the swing.

6

Curing Faults

Ben Hogan once pointed out that the ultimate readout on your swing is the flight of the ball. In curing faults, you've got to learn to look at your ball flight critically in the initial direction in which the ball flies and any subsequent curve and height level. These factors will tell you what happened during your swing.

It's important to realize that there are only two ways to hit a ball crooked; either your swing plane is off or your clubface is not square at impact.

To understand what the swing plane is, imagine that you're standing to the right of a golfer addressing a ball with good, square alignment. Then visualize a huge disk with a hole in the middle of it. The disk rests on the player's shoulders, with his head through the hole and the lower edge of the disk going through the middle of the ball. During the swing, the clubhead should follow the outer edge of the disk back and through.

In order for the clubhead to do this, the shoulders must return to a position square (or parallel to the target line) at impact; then the arms and hands can swing the club through the ball on the target line.

However, if the shoulders are open at impact, this tilts the whole disk to the player's left, and as a result the arms and hands swing the club from outside the target line to inside across the ball. The ball then starts to the left of straight. Conversely, if the shoulders are closed at impact, the disk tilts to the right and the clubhead swings through the ball from inside the target line to outside, and the ball starts to the right of straight.

Whether the ball continues to travel straight in relation to your swing plane depends on whether your clubface is square, open or closed at impact in relation to the swing plane. Here are the various possibilities.

1. *Shoulders square at impact, and plane correct.*
   a. Clubface square to the plane at impact: ball goes straight.
   b. Clubface open to the plane at impact: ball starts straight, but slices to the right.
   c. Clubface closed to the plane at impact: ball starts straight, then hooks to the left.

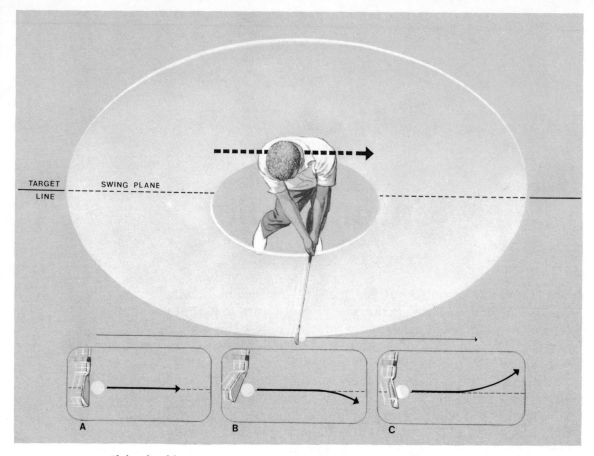

TARGET LINE   SWING PLANE

A   B   C

45. If the shoulders are square to the target line at impact, the swing plane is correct. If the clubface is square to the swing plane (A), the ball flies straight. If the clubface is open (B), the ball starts straight but then slices to the right. If the clubface is closed (C), the ball starts straight but then hooks to the left.

46. *Above right.* If the shoulders are open to the target line at impact, then the swing plane is tilted to the left. If the clubface is square to the swing plane (A), the ball flies straight left (a pull). If the clubface is open (B), the ball starts left but slices back to the right (pull/slice). If the clubface is closed, the ball starts left and hooks farther left (pull/hook).

47. *Below right.* If the shoulders are closed to the target line at impact, then the swing plane is tilted to the right. If the clubface is square to the swing plane (A), the ball flies straight right (a push). If the clubface is open (B), the ball starts right but slices farther right (push/slice). If the clubface is closed (C), the ball starts right and then hooks back to the left (push/hook).

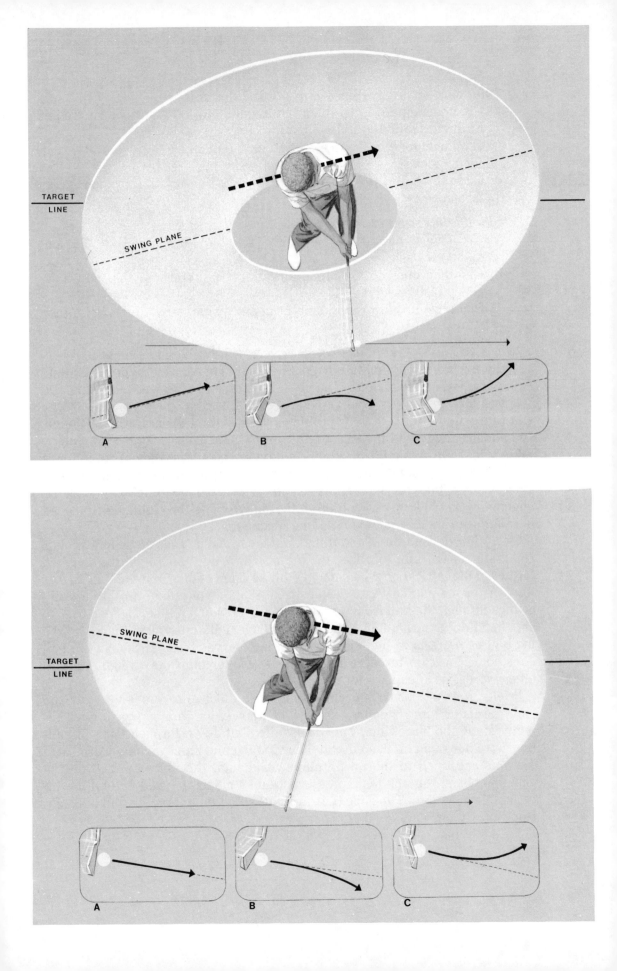

TARGET
LINE

SWING PLANE

A   B   C

SWING PLANE

TARGET
LINE

A   B   C

2. ***Shoulders open at impact, and plane tilted left.***
   a. Clubface square to the plane at impact: ball goes straight to the left of target (called a pull).
   b. Clubface open to the plane at impact: ball starts to the left of target, then slices.
   c. Clubface closed to the plane at impact: ball starts left, then hooks farther left.

3. ***Shoulders closed at impact, and plane tilted right.***
   a. Clubface square to the plane at impact: ball goes straight to the right (called a push).
   b. Clubface open to the plane at impact: ball starts to the right, then slices farther right.
   c. Clubface closed to the plane at impact: ball starts to the right, then hooks back.

When you're hitting crooked, you have to study the ball's flight and proceed by a process of elimination. As Sherlock Holmes used to do, you eliminate possibilities one by one. Then what remains is what you're looking for.

If you merely rely on your instincts, which is what most golfers do, you will probably only make your problems worse. As a general rule of thumb, you should always do the exact *opposite* of what your instincts tell you.

Let's take an example of a very common fault, the slice. The golfer is hitting the ball straight, but it curves to the right toward the end of its flight. Let's assume that the golfer has set up with a good address and square alignment. So we know now that all that is wrong is the clubface—it's open in relation to the correct swing plane at impact.

Our golfer doesn't think about that, however. All he sees is the ball slicing. His instincts tell him to allow for the curve in the ball's flight by aligning farther to the left. So now he sets up with an open stance and the ball farther forward in the stance. As a result, he tilts his swing plane to the left and swings through the ball from out to in, with an open clubface. He also tries to stay behind it to straighten out the shot. His last state is worse than the first: the ball now starts to the left of target, then curves back. Although the ball does come back on target, a pull/slice is weaker than the straight shot. In other words, he's losing a lot of distance.

Briefly, here's why: When you swing from out to in, across the ball, the club descends more steeply on the ball than when you swing through directly along the target line. This drives the club down through the ball, putting more backspin on it, so that it flies too high and stops quickly. Also, with the clubface open to the swing plane at impact, the ball is struck only a glancing blow. You don't compress the ball as much as when you hit it with the clubface square. The slice (left-to-right) spin you put on the ball makes it stop quickly on landing.

Let's see how you could tackle the problem with what I've told you. You see the ball is flying straight, then curving to the right toward the end of the flight. Apparently, your swing plane is fine, but you check anyway. You first check your ball position. To do that, you run your eye from the blade to your left heel, and see that it's correct. You check your alignment by putting down two clubs parallel to the target line—one just on the far side of the ball, the other across your toes. Then you check your hip and shoulder alignment by placing the shaft of a club across your hips and then your shoulders. A third check is to hit some balls with a 5-iron. If the divot starts straight toward the target before coming back to the inside, then you know that not only are you setting up the correct swing plane at address, but also that the swing plane is correct at impact.

So now you know, through the process of elimination, that all that is wrong is the clubface—it's slightly open to the swing plane at impact. There are only a few possible causes: You could be setting up with the clubface open to the target line. Your clubface could be square but your grip too weak (V's, say, to the left of the chin), and at impact your hands are returning to their natural position (turned more to the right), opening the clubface. Finally, your clubface could be square at address, but you're not releasing the club properly through impact—too much pulling with the left arm, not enough rotation of the left forearm and hand to the left. The solutions are to square the clubface at the target, with the leading edge at right angles to the target; take a stronger grip than you have been doing, the correct, square grip, and rotate the club shaft with the left arm through impact, working the blade from toe up halfway down to toe up halfway through.

A lot of beginners feel more powerful if they're set up well behind the ball. As a result, they play the ball much too far forward. Obviously when you do that, your hips and shoulders open, you tilt the swing plane to the left, and you cut across the ball at impact. You pull straight to the left or pull/slice, the ball starting left and slicing back to the right. So if you're getting this type of ball flight, first get the ball back in the correct place in the stance, and square the shoulders and feet to the target line. Then, if you're still slicing, apply the solutions above.

In the same way that a slicer's instincts tell him to align his body farther to the left and play the ball farther forward in the stance, the player who is hooking the ball will tend to do the exact opposite. He'll try to allow for the hook by aligning farther to the right and playing the ball farther back in the stance. He ends with the swing plane tilted to the right, and swings through the ball from in to out with closed clubface. The ball then starts to the right and hooks back to the left, a push/hook.

If you get to the point where you're push/hooking, first get the ball farther forward in the correct position so that you can square up your shoulders and hips. Then correct the clubface problem if you're still hooking.

Among my own children, John, Jr., tends to play the ball too far forward.

However, Scott, my second-oldest boy, has a tendency that is more difficult for golfers to spot. He doesn't swing up and down on the swing plane established at address. Rather, he swings back on one plane and through on another.

Scott sets up with his body aligned to the right of target. His swing plane is tilted to the right, and you would expect that he would push/hook, as previously described. What he actually does is "come over the top of the ball" in the forward swing, with the right shoulder working more around the body than under the chin. This shifts his swing plane to more or less the correct position at impact, but often his clubface is closed in relation to the swing plane, and he hits the ball low, at best, and often hooks it.

This type of swing problem underlines the importance of checking your alignment and ball position first, whatever the type of crooked shot you're hitting. If they are incorrect, yet it appears that you're swinging through on the correct plane, then you know that you've got a "loop" in your swing. If you're setting up to the right of target, you're swinging back to the inside and then looping "over the top" along the target line. If you're setting up left, then you're taking it back outside the line, then looping back inside to swing the club down the line.

So often, the golfer is the last one to realize that his alignment is off. If you're in any doubt, ask a buddy to stand to your right at address and tell you where you're aiming, or ask your pro—his trained eyes can spot such flaws in a second.

OTHER SWING FLAWS

Unfortunately, not all swing flaws result in a crooked shot. Instead, they give you a variety of mishits. Here are some of the more common faults that beginners have, along with the types of mishit that usually accompany them.

Tension. If you're striking the ball solidly and straight but you're losing a bit of distance, usually the reason is tension in your hands, arms and body. This prevents you from getting maximum speed through the ball. Lighten your grip with the "little bird" image I gave you earlier. Also, make sure that your arms are hanging down at address and you can feel the weight of the club in your hands as you set up and waggle.

Sway Back, Sway Through. This fault is particularly common among younger children up to the age of ten or so. They don't have much strength and the club feels heavy or is too heavy for them. They feel they can get more power by allowing the whole body to sway to the right going back and then sway to the left through the ball. (In other words, they don't make a good turn—mainly just a slide to the right and a slide back to the left.) This results in a variety of mishits. If they don't sway back to the ball enough in

48. The reverse weight shift is a most destructive fault. Instead of shifting the weight to the right foot in the backswing, you shift it to the left foot. Coming down, you react by shifting the weight to the right foot. Most often, you hit "fat," that is, behind the ball.

the downswing, the low point of the swing is behind the ball, and they can hit the ground behind the ball (hitting "fat," as it is called). If they sway past the ball in the downswing, they can push the ball to the right or they can contact the top half of the ball, hitting low and thin, or even smothering it. The correction is to coil and turn against the right leg going back, preventing the sway. Putting a wedge of wood under the outside edge of the right foot also is a very good corrective drill.

49–52. *Across.* Ben Hogan is a perfect model for the key move at the start of the down-swing. See the way his arms drop as the shoulders stay back. When the hands are about hip high, he lets the arms and body fly through the ball.

Reverse Weight Shift. If you set up at address with too much weight on your left foot, what usually happens in the backswing is that you leave too much weight on your left foot, and react in the downswing by shifting the weight to your right foot. This is the exact opposite of the correct weight shift —that's why it's called the "reverse weight shift." It's also possible to set up correctly and then shift the weight to your left foot, rather than your right, going back.

Either way, the weight is on your right foot in the downswing. This moves the low point of the swing behind the ball. Most often, you hit the ball "fat," but you can also have the blade bounce off the ground behind the ball and then strike the top half of the ball, topping or thinning it. Sometimes, you can get lucky and "drop kick" the blade right into the back of the ball so that it flies pretty well.

The correction is to set up with the weight correctly divided between your feet and to shift the weight to your right foot in the backswing.

Hitting from the Top. I've touched on this earlier, but the early hit is so common among beginners, it's well worth treating it more thoroughly here. In fact, it's John, Jr.'s, biggest problem—I constantly work on it with him. What happens is this: You want to get power, so you start hitting from the top of the backswing. You immediately release your right shoulder, the angle in your right arm and the angle in your wrists between the club and your left arm. This causes a tremendous power loss.

I liken hitting from the top to an automobile that's halted for a stop sign. If you "floor" the gas pedal quickly, all you'll do, especially with a powerful car, is sit there, burning tire rubber. However, if you come off the line and gradually depress the gas pedal, you'll be more efficient. You'll get more power and better fuel economy.

It's the same way in the golf swing. At the change of direction of the swing, ideally there's a zero mph point as the club comes to a momentary stop. You can't accelerate a car from zero to 60 mph in one second, and you can't accelerate the club quickly from the top of the swing. Instead, you've got to allow the arms and club to catch up with the shoulders, leaving the shoulders passive in the first half of the downswing as you drive the knees laterally.

The Downswing. The biggest problem in the downswing is that your arms have to move through a bigger circle than your body. If you move your shoulders and hips as fast as your arms from the top of the swing, your body is way open to the target line by the time your hands reach hip height, and you slice the ball.

Instead, you should feel as though your knees are driving laterally and your shoulders are staying back (not turning) as your arms drop. Then, when your hands reach hip height, your arms will have caught up with the body action, and you can let your body and arms fly through impact at the same speed. Although I haven't talked to Ben Hogan myself about this "shoulders back, arms drop" move, I've been told by several people who know him well that he feels that this is the secret to his swing.

In closing this chapter on common faults, I want to give you another reason for keeping notebooks on your game listing the faults you commonly make. Most players have faults that they tend to make time and time again. If you note them, then you can more easily cure them in the future.

7

Swing Variations

I favor a simple swing, in which the player adopts a square grip and a square setup and the clubhead follows the same, correct plane back and through. The less complicated you keep the swing, the less there is to go wrong.

The golfer I used to illustrate the seven key positions in Chapter 5, Jack Nicklaus, has such a swing. Smooth, rhythmic and powerful, it has long been the standard against which other swings are judged. (The sequence was taken in 1973, when Nicklaus was thirty-three years old.)

Nicklaus' first victory as a professional came in his first year on Tour, 1962. Appropriately, it was a "major" championship, the U.S. Open. I say "appropriately" because Nicklaus has set a record for winning the most majors—twenty—that may never be equaled. Here's his tally: six Masters, five PGA Championships, four U.S. Opens, three British Opens and two U.S. Amateurs. He has seventy-one victories on the PGA Tour, including two in his own tournament, the Memorial, in 1977 and 1984.

I could go on, but the point I want to make is that this simple swing is one that you can use throughout your life. The "proof of the pudding" is Nicklaus' career. Now in his forties, he is still going strong.

As I said earlier, however, many of the top players use variations of this basic swing, I among them. As you develop your own swing, you may favor one of these variations. If you do, these photos provide you with model swings to emulate.

In general, I have chosen pictures of each golfer in the seven key positions. In this way, you can compare one swing with another. In some cases, I've deviated slightly to show points I haven't yet covered.

VARIATIONS IN WRIST ACTION

There are three types of wrist action. There is the "early set," of which I (6 ft. 3 in., 185 lbs.) am an example. There is the "natural set," used by Nicklaus (5 ft. 11 in., 180 lbs.). Finally, there is the "delayed set," which

Bobby Clampett (5 ft. 10 in., 146 lbs.) employs. They are distinctly different, yet all of them are good.

Early Set. In my swing, my wrists break naturally in the takeaway. By about midway in the backswing, I've completed my wrist cock. My wrists stay in the same position until I'm halfway down, then I uncock them in the hitting area, mirroring the action in the backswing.

This sequence was taken in 1974, when I was at the pinnacle of my success. This is my finest swing, the one that won the '73 U.S. Open, and eight tournaments in 1974.

Natural Set. In Nicklaus' swing, there is some wrist cock at the start of the backswing, but less than in my swing. (Compare the second picture of each swing.) Most of the wrist action occurs between halfway back and the top of the swing. There is approximately a 10 percent increase in wrist cock in the first move down, which helps keep the transition from backswing to downswing smooth and fluid. It gives Nicklaus time to plant his left heel so he can hit against his left side.

These sequence photos were taken just before Nicklaus came on Tour in 1962. He then was 30 pounds heavier than he is today. Note that in this early sequence his right foot is turned more to the right at address than it is later. Turning the right foot out gives one a bigger body turn. In both sequences, his left foot is turned to the left at address, but in the first move down, he plants it more squarely to the target line (in this sequence) and square to the target line in the '73 sequence. This makes certain that he swings the club down into the ball from the inside. An interesting move. Other points to study are the height of his hands at the top, aided by his famous "flying right elbow," the right arm leaving the side more than with other top players, and the power in Nicklaus' legs. In my experience in studying golfers, this is the most awesome power swing ever to strike a golf ball.

This swing shows Nicklaus' upbringing in the game. As a youngster, he was taught to hit the ball as hard as he could. Then, as he got older, he modified his swing for more control. In contrast, I was taught super basic fundamentals as a youngster, then my swing got longer and more powerful as I got older.

Delayed Set. In Bobby Clampett's swing, there is very little wrist cock in the takeaway, and some between halfway back and the top. However, the big difference here is that his wrists aren't fully cocked until the first position shown in the downswing. Then he uncocks them through the ball.

This delayed set produces an action called "snap loading." There's no stress on the shaft going back, but then you put tremendous stress on the shaft coming down with the snap loading, which is like cracking a whip.

The delayed set does generate tremendous power. That's why some of the smaller players, such as Gary Player and Lanny Wadkins, use this method. However, of the three types of wrist action, it is the most difficult to time, because so much of the wrist action takes place in the downswing, where the club is moving fastest.

This sequence was taken in 1979, when Clampett was nineteen years old. At the time, he was literally a golfing machine from tee to green.

VARIATIONS IN ALIGNMENT

Although I advocate setting up with the clubface and body squarely aligned to the target, not every top golfer does this. Al Geiberger (6 ft. 2 in., 185 lbs.) sets up slightly open. Sam Snead (5 ft. 11 in., 185 lbs.) sets up a trifle closed. I've included my own swing here for comparison, as my alignment is square.

Open Alignment. I had to find a spot in this book for "Mr. 59," because I think he owns one of the best swings out on Tour. (Geiberger became the first player to break 60 in an official Tour event when he won the 1977 Memphis Classic.) If you want to copy one swing, copy his. It's the simplest I've seen.

He sets up with very good posture, his body aligned to the left edge of the fairway, his clubface aligned to the target, which is to the right of his intended swing plane. He then makes a pure swing—no manipulation of the blade—and a pure release. Every position is letter-perfect. The result is a fade that starts to the left, where his feet are aimed, and then drifts back to the right to his target.

Another reason Geiberger fades is that his shoulders stay "in sync" with his arms so well through the ball. If you want to fade, a good key is a dominant but smooth shoulder movement through the ball. An aid here is to grip a bit firmer with the left hand. This tightens the left arm and shoulder muscles a little, and that shortens the backswing slightly. Then your arms can trail your shoulders through the hitting area, producing a fade.

This sequence was taken in 1971, when Geiberger was forty-four years old.

Square Alignment. I set up with my shoulders square to the target line, clubface at the hole. My swing demonstrates several checkpoints for being on plane. At the top, the club shaft is parallel to the target line. Also, a line drawn down my left arm points at the ball. A third checkpoint is that a line drawn across the clubface should point straight down at the ball. Mine actually points down a little inside the ball. The clubface is slightly open, which you would expect with my weak grip. In Position Four, the club shaft points straight down at the ball. This is the position you must be in to be on plane. That's why it's the most important position besides impact. Get Position Four right, and your chances of being correct at impact are very good. At impact, note how my right forearm is in line with the shaft.

53–59. *Across.* EARLY SET: In my swing, I've completed my wrist cock about halfway into the backswing. I keep my wrists cocked until I reach a point halfway in the downswing, then I uncock them in the hitting area.

60–66. *Across*. NATURAL SET: Jack Nicklaus uses some wrist cock in the takeaway but less than in my swing (compare our "halfway back" positions). Most of the cocking action occurs between halfway back and the top.

67–73. *Across.* DELAYED SET: Bobby
Clampett has very little wrist cock
in the takeaway, and some between halfway back and the top.
However, his wrists aren't fully
cocked until the first position
shown in the downswing.

74–80. *Across.* OPEN ALIGNMENT: Al Geiberger sets up with his body aligned to the left of his target but aims his clubface to the right of his body alignment. The ball starts to the left, then fades back to the target.

81–87. *Across.* SQUARE ALIGNMENT: I
set up with a square alignment: my
feet, hips and shoulders parallel to
the target line. The club shaft is
parallel to the target line at the top;
in Position Four, it points at the
ball.

88–94. *Across.* CLOSED ALIGNMENT: Sam Snead has set his feet and shoulders well to the right of his target, so that his swing plane is to the right. Coming through the ball, his right arm crosses the left, creating a draw.

When you have pictures taken of your swing, always have some taken from this angle as well as from the front, so that you can check out these points.

Closed Alignment. If you can set the ball down the right side of the fairway and really release the club, you get a draw, the longest type of shot, with the most roll. This is what Sam Snead does so well. There's an out-of-bounds just left of the fairway on this hole (the first at Riviera), so Snead is aiming farther right than usual. He has set his feet and shoulders at the tree line, intending to draw the ball back to the middle of the fairway.

In photo 2, he has come back inside the plane a little, but then he swings upward, and is right on plane at the top.

Through the ball, Snead shows a typical draw/hook action; his shoulders follow the arms through. The reason you draw the ball is that your arms catch up with your shoulders at impact. The shoulders almost stop being dominant. The right arm crosses the left—and there's your draw.

If you want to draw the ball consistently, tell your big shoulder muscles to relax and let your hands and forearms do more of the work. If anything, grip the club a little lighter than usual; that will make your arms and hands move faster.

This sequence was taken in 1973, when Sneed was sixty-one years old.

A MODEL SWING

Jane Blalock's Swing. Blalock's swing is a wonderful model for anyone— boy as well as girl. She does use a slightly stronger grip than I recommend, but other than that, I rate her swing as near perfect. In Position Two, she has a slight amount of wrist break. She sets the club faster than Nicklaus, but much less quickly than I do—a very good, neutral position. At the top, study the angle between the left arm and the club: it's a little less than 90 degrees. In the fourth photo, this angle has increased to about 100 degrees. This is a tremendous angle and is due to her fine leg action leading the downswing. She's actually doing a little snap loading. At impact, note how her left shoulder, her arm and the shaft are dead in line, as they were at address. Also, as with the other great players shown, note that the shaft is pointing up straight between her legs; this proves the hit was perfectly timed. In Position Five, she's kept her left wrist very firm—she may have cupped it just a little, but still this is a fine position. In the follow-through, she shows perfect balance, with her weight on her left side.

This sequence was shot in 1974, when Blalock was twenty-eight years old.

THE ULTIMATE GOLFER

Sam Snead once told me, "Son, you're either going to hit the long shots well, or middle and short irons well." At the time, this didn't make much sense to me, but today I firmly believe he was right.

Most golfers' swings do fall into one or the other category: they're either good in the long game and not so good in the middle and short games, or vice versa.

When Jack Nicklaus first came out on Tour, he was known for his awesome length, and as the greatest 1-, 2- and 3-iron player ever, but his short-iron game left much to be desired. At the other end of the scale, I've been known for years as one of the best middle- to short-iron players in the world. With anything from a 4-iron to a wedge in my hand, I hit the ball so close to the hole it sometimes makes people shake their heads.

To understand why this is so, you have to go back to basics, in particular the grip.

With a strong grip, the left thumb in the 2 o'clock position, you tend to take the club back in a wide, sweeping motion. You also get a lot of side-to-side movement in the swing: you move to the right going back and to the left coming through. If you looked at the arc of the swing, the path traced by the clubhead when viewed from the front, it would be closer to an ellipse (like looking at the length of a football lying on its side) than a circle. The flattened portion of the arc through the ball is ideal for driving the ball forward, making this a powerful type of action in the long game. It widens the arc.

There's a snag, however, to the strong grip. At address, you create an angle in the back of the left hand, and as you go into your takeaway, it's pretty much instinctive to straighten the left wrist. This closes the clubface by the top of the swing.

In the downswing, you have to make a big lateral movement of the legs and lead the clubhead with a firm left hand to keep the clubface square at impact. You don't release as consistently through impact with a strong grip. Indeed, if you did release and rotate, you would hook the ball. This "hang on tight with the left hand" action leads to a fade like Trevino's and Lietzke's.

Another snag with the strong grip is evident in iron play. If you overdo the lateral move with your legs and the lead of your hands in front of the clubhead—and under pressure this can happen fairly often—your club shaft leans farther forward at impact than it was at address. The handle is farther ahead of the clubhead, reducing the effective loft of the club. Your impact position becomes too variable. If you're hitting a 7-iron, you can put 6- or 5-iron loft on the ball, rather than 7-iron loft. Your distance control is bad.

The golfers who complain about "hitting the ball pure" but flying over a lot of greens are invariably golfers with strong grips.

95–101. *Across.* A MODEL SWING: Jane Blalock has a great swing. In the fourth photo, note the tremendous angle between the left arm and the club shaft. By impact, she's released this angle, while keeping the left wrist very firm.

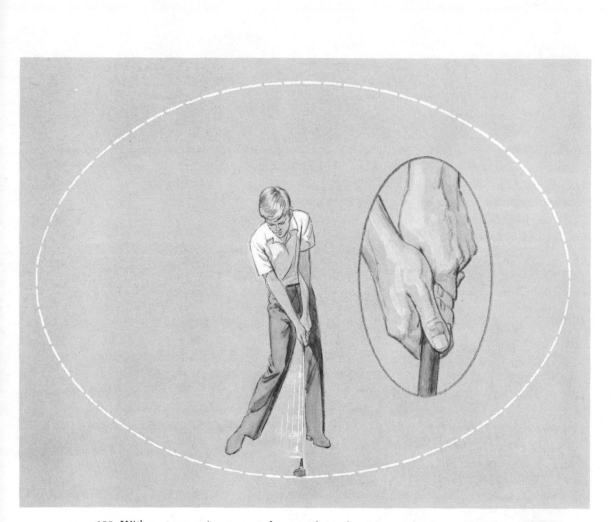

102. With a strong grip, you get the most lateral movement in the swing. You get a big, wide, sweeping arc that's ideal in the long game. However, with irons your distance control can be bad.

If you adopt a square grip (the left thumb in the 1 o'clock position), you can develop a swing that is ideal for the long game. Yet it has none of the disadvantages of the strong grip. You can still make a big, wide, sweeping backswing and a big football-shaped arc. With the square grip, you can keep the left wrist straight throughout the swing—you don't close the clubface as much as with the strong grip. You can then drive your legs hard in the downswing and still release the club properly through the ball. You get all the speed out of the proper release of the angles of the right arm and wrist, as well as the rotation of the right forearm over the left.

You have an option in regard to the height of the arc. You can copy Jack Nicklaus' swing and let the right elbow "fly" a little going back, allowing the

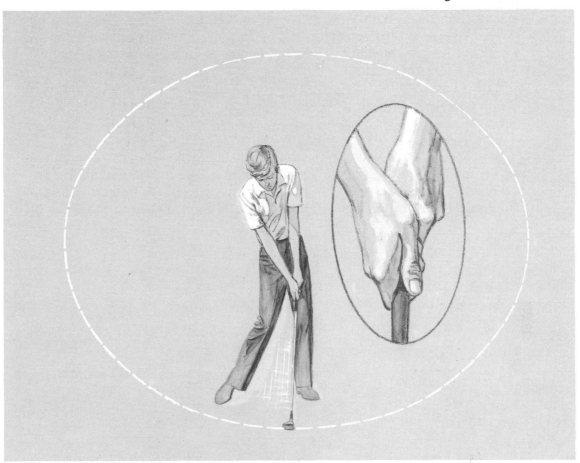

103. With a square grip, you still get almost as big an arc as with the strong grip. It's excellent for your long game. However, in the short game, you tend to get high, floating shots because you're sweeping the ball.

elbow to come away from the side so that the hands and club reach the height they do above Nicklaus' head. This height of arc gives you greater leverage in the downswing. However, you do need strong and active legs to make this method work—Jack's leg muscles are probably the strongest muscles in his body. If you find the method difficult, then emulate Sam Snead's action, in which the right arm folds into the side of the body going back, resulting in a slightly lower hand and club position and flatter swing plane (than Nicklaus').

Nicklaus' swing is probably the ultimate power swing, but Snead's is good too.

When you try to take the power swing into the short game, you will find that it's not ideal. With the ball up off the left heel, you get high, floating shots, because you're sweeping the ball up. This method is good for the wood and longer irons, but there's not enough spin on the shots for control with the short irons.

With a high shot into the green, you're always a "bluebird" player. You're fine in good weather, but if there's a wind, the ball is liable to be blown off course.

I've asked a lot of youngsters what the shape of the trajectory should be with a short iron, and most of them say, "A nice high arc, a ball that drops on the green." That's a special shot you can play, as we'll see in the short-game chapter, but it's not the ideal standard shot. A good short iron should be hit

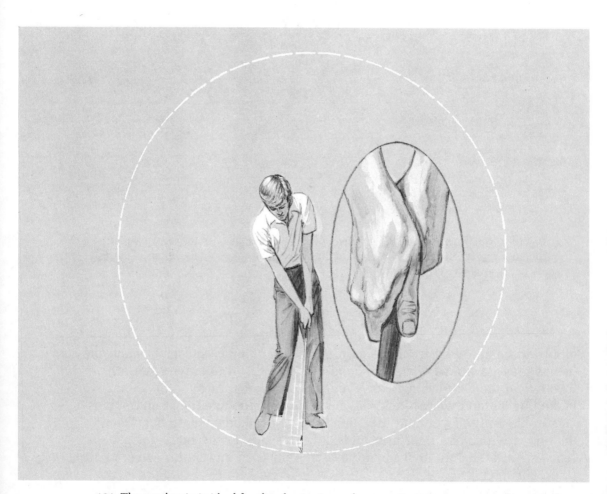

104. The weak grip is ideal for the shorter irons, because it encourages an early set and a more circular arc—there's much less lateral action. You get very good distance control.

with a firm, descending blow, so that the ball is trapped on the clubface and has a lower flight, with plenty of backspin.

The way you get this correct flight with the short irons is to play the ball back more in the middle of the stance, take a quicker wrist break (early set) so that you hit the ball firmly, and hit through impact with a straight and very firm left wrist.

This is where the "weak" grip (left thumb at 12 o'clock) comes into play. The grip encourages more of an early set. There's much less lateral movement with the "weak grip" swing. It's more of a turn of the body to the right as the arms swing the club up and the wrists break upward, then another turn of the body through as you swing the club down with the arms and the wrists uncock. After impact the wrists break upward. There's very little, if any, lateral (side-to-side) cocking in the weak-grip swing. You swing the club up and down and up again in an arc that is almost a perfect circle. Because the club comes up quicker in the finish than in the square- or the strong-grip swing, you're encouraged to play the ball farther back in the stance and get that firm, descending blow that traps the ball on the clubface.

With the weak grip, the angle in the left wrist remains almost constant during the swing, and with less lateral leg action in the downswing, the club shaft is virtually at the same angle (when viewed from the front) at address and at impact (check the pictures of my swing). Whatever the loft of the club you're using, that's the loft you put on the ball. This, incidentally, is why I hit my irons with such consistent distance. If I hit the ball straight and solid, I *know* the ball is close to the pin.

The ultimate golfer, therefore, would be one who used a 1 o'clock grip in the long game and a big, wide swing that resembled Nicklaus' or Snead's swing. He would use a 12 o'clock grip from the 4-iron down through the wedges, as I do, and work on a more circular, up-and-down swing that gave crisp, accurate shots.

You shouldn't try the 12 o'clock grip in the middle and short irons until you've reached fifteen or sixteen years old or have developed strong hands and forearms. Until then, use the 1 o'clock grip.

Interestingly, Nicklaus has modified his short-iron play. He went to Phil Rodgers and started working on moving the ball back in his stance with the short irons and using a faster wrist break in the backswing. He also has weakened his left-hand grip.

I must admit that I have been trying to go to a 1 o'clock grip in my long game recently, and the results have been very encouraging. I wish I had tried that ten years ago—maybe it's not too late.

8

The Art of Shot Making

Of the young players I see on the PGA Tour, ninety-five percent either hit hard, straight balls or can only put one kind of sidespin on the ball (either hook spin or slice spin). In most cases, they don't vary the speed of the swing to control distance. I call them "one shot" golfers.

I don't think these players will ever be complete golfers, in that they will never be able to cope with all the different types of courses and conditions. To do that, you must be a shot maker, able to vary how hard and far you hit the ball and to curve the ball to the left or right.

Only a few of the shots you hit are normal full shots. If you hit a 4-iron 180 yards and a 5-iron 170 yards, what do you do when you have 175 yards to the pin? If you want to play the Tour one day, or even if you just want to be a good amateur, it's not good enough to say "I'll hit a full 4-iron or 5-iron," because either way you're facing a 15-foot putt—even if you hit the ball dead straight. You have to be able to create a shot that is correct for the distance within a yard or two.

One way to vary yardage is to learn how to put a little extra on a straight shot by swinging a little harder or take something off it by swinging a little easier. The other way is to draw (a slight hook) or fade (a slight slice). If your normal, straight 5-iron goes 170 yards, then a drawn 5-iron will go, say, five yards farther, and a faded 5-iron about five yards less. When you can combine the two techniques you literally have a shot for every distance. This is what I do, and that's one reason why I'm known for hitting the ball close. Drawing and fading the ball is also a percentage shot when the pin is tucked behind a bunker on the left or right of the green. When the pin's tucked left, play a draw that hits the middle of the green and then kicks left toward the pin. If the shot comes off, your ball is far closer to the hole than if you hit a straight shot for the middle of the green. If it doesn't hook, you still have the middle of the green locked up. When the pin's tucked right, you can fade the ball into the flag.

Before we start on shot making, there are a few more things I would like to touch on first.

105. When the pin is tucked behind a bunker on the left of the green, hit a draw that lands in the middle of the green. Then the ball will kick left close to the pin.

106. When the pin is tucked behind a bunker on the right of the green, the percentage shot is to hit a fade that lands in the middle of the green and kicks right toward the hole.

Before the age of twelve, you usually aren't strong enough to spin the ball to the right or left more than a few yards. However you hit it, it pretty much stays on line. You also can't put much backspin on the ball—you can't, for example, hit an iron shot that backs up. You should work on distance control solely by how hard you swing.

The way to tell that you're old enough to learn shot making is to study your bad shots. If you sometimes slice a ball twenty yards, you're putting enough spin on the ball. You're ready.

Another requirement is that you can hit the ball reasonably straight. If there's a secret to shot making, it is that the various shots are simply slight modifications of the straight ball. So if you pull/slice the ball, for example, you must correct your swing first.

Thirdly, you must know how far you hit each club in your bag. In practice or on the course, pace off the distances. Eventually, you'll know the distance you can normally expect from each club, and how the various shots affect it.

HARD AND SOFT SHOTS

To learn how to hit the ball a little harder or more easily than usual, take a 5-iron out to the practice tee and try to get at least a 10-yard variance in distance. Say your normal distance is 170 yards. Try to swing a little harder than usual and get another five yards. Then gradually ease back on your tempo, until you're hitting the ball only 160 yards or so. This is a good variance in distance.

To aid in varying your swing speed, use your imagination. Say your clubhead speed on a normal 5-iron is 83 mph.* Hit a few full 5-irons to register that speed in your mind. Then hit a few more swinging a little harder—call that 85 mph. Then, much in the same way as you did when establishing your "red line," note the distance you get with 85 mph, and as you throttle back, assign lower speeds to each swing, again noting the distance you get in each case. Eventually, you reach the point where you can dial in an 80 or 82 mph swing and know how much less distance you get with each speed.

When I was growing up, my imagination was the only tool I had to work with. I must say I haven't done too badly with it. However, today there are swing computers that tell you your clubhead speed at impact. (I use "Sport Tech." It's great.) So the ideal way to work on swing speed would be with one of these computers. You can check your actual clubhead speed at impact against how it feels. My experience with these machines shows that checking your feel of clubhead speed against the fact of the computer can be very helpful. Soon, almost everyone will have access to such computers.

When you're working on swing speed, remember that that is *all* you're

---

* The speeds given are my speeds with a 5-iron.

working on. You don't need to choke down on the club or swing back shorter than usual. I find that if you choke down on a full iron shot, you get such a good connection on the club, that you often hit as far as a full shot. Also, if you take a short backswing, you tend to rush the tempo and jerk the club down from the top, ruining the shot. Swing fully on each shot, and alter only the tempo. It's by far the more reliable method.

This isn't something that only I do. Far from it. When I was in my teens, Dutch Harrison was the pro at the Olympic Club in San Francisco. Dutch won twenty Tour events from the '30s to the '50s and was known for his soft shots. I used to hear tales of his taking young Tour pros out on practice rounds and driving them crazy with these shots. Typically, the stories went something like this:

Dutch and the young pro came to a par 3 hole. Say it was 170 yards with water over the green. Dutch would take a 3-iron and put a big, syrupy swing on the ball, which dropped softly by the pin. Then the young pro, who had been fingering a 5-iron, didn't know what to do. He'd most likely change to a 4-iron and fly the ball right over the green into the water.

I confuse a lot of the other pros on the Tour when they hawk my bag, because I do the same sort of thing. They can see the club I'm hitting, but what they don't know is that I'm swinging a little harder or more softly than on a normal full shot. In fact, it never occurs to them, because all they know is how to hit the ball with one, full speed.

I should point out that soft shots are not only for the times you're "in between" clubs. You should know that when you hit a shot hard, you get maximum backspin on the ball. However, there are times when too much backspin can hurt you. A good example is the seventh hole at Pebble Beach, where the green tilts toward you. I see a lot of young pros come to this hole, hit a short iron hard, land next to the hole and backspin twenty feet short. They say, "Jeez, what a bad break I got." They didn't have a bad break—they just hit the wrong kind of shot.

What they don't realize is that, in such a situation, you should take one more club, grip it lightly and then hit the ball in slow motion. With less backspin, the ball hits and sticks—it won't even back up.

A good time to take the weaker of the two clubs is when you're in a clutch situation and you're pumped up to the point where you're going to hit harder anyway. If you take the stronger club and try to swing easily, you might "jump" at it and barrel right over the green. Funnily enough, though, I'm an exception to this rule. Pressure doesn't affect me this way. I hit the ball exactly the same distance as usual. So you have to know yourself in this regard.

The more slowly you want to swing, the lighter you grip the club, and the slower you swing your arms. Going along with the slower arm swing is the right leg action. For a slow arm swing, think of "soft" knees, your legs working gently back and through. "Soft" knees tend to trigger "soft," slowly moving arms. Conversely, when you want to hit the ball hard, your right leg must be very firm as you make a big turn behind the ball. Coil deeply into the leg, so that it resists the turn. Then the right leg fires more vigorously halfway down and helps you swing the arms faster through the ball.

I started showing my son John, Jr., how to vary the pace of his swing when he was twelve years old. He's taken to it like a duck to water. Already he can play shots that many young men on the Tour don't even try.

CURVE BALLS

I've said that learning to curve the ball can enable you to work the ball into a pin that is tucked behind a bunker. It also allows you to dial in a more exact distance on a particular iron. To show you how this works out in practice, here's a tournament situation in which I did both of these things on one shot.

I was playing in the '74 Phoenix Open. As I came to my ball to play my second shot at the 17th hole, I heard a roar from the gallery on 18 which meant that Lanny Wadkins had sunk his putt for an eagle 3. I knew what I had to do: to tie him, I had to par 17 and birdie 18, or vice versa. My caddie and I agreed that I had exactly 165 yards to the pin. Now, my normal 5-iron is good for 170 yards, my 6-iron 160. So I was "in between" clubs. However, because the hole was tucked on the right side of the green, I elected to play a faded 5-iron, relying on the fade to take the five yards off the normal distance. The shot came off exactly as I visualized it, the ball starting ten feet left of the pin, fading back to the right, hitting the green five feet left of the hole and then spinning to the right. It finished six inches away. I then went on to birdie the last hole and won the tournament.

Before I get to the specifics of playing curve balls, let me say that there are two ways to play them: the hard way and the easy way. Many teachers would have you believe that you must change your grip, your stance, and even your normal swing plane. I don't believe in such methods, because you run the risk of losing the groove of your swing just to play one shot. For example, say you had played a slice by "swinging more outside in." You might step up to your next tee shot and slice it with the same action, even though you didn't want to.

In my method, I believe in changing as little as possible.

FADES AND SLICES

To make a ball curve to the right, the clubface has to be open to (aimed to the right of) the swing plane at impact. The clubhead then hits the ball, and the ball slides off the open face with left-to-right spin.

To fade or slice the ball, the technique is the same. You set up as though you were going to hit an imaginary target to the left of the actual target, your shoulders, hips and feet aligned left, where you want the ball to start, but you aim the leading edge of the blade at the actual target. Because you swing along the path established by your shoulders, hips and feet, your swing plane is tilted to the left. However, the clubface is open in relation to the swing plane at impact, so you put the necessary left-to-right spin on the ball. The ball starts to the left, a little to the right of the line you swing through the ball, then curves back to the right.

As a general rule, the ball starts its flight in the direction of the swing path through impact. However, when you fade or slice the ball, the ball tends to

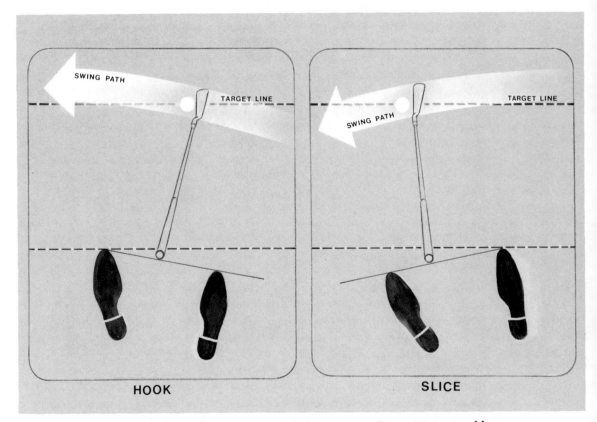

107. To hook or slice the ball, you need only make minor changes in your address position. To hook the ball, set up as though you were going to hit to an imaginary target to the right of the actual target, but close the clubface, aiming the leading edge of the club at the actual target. You swing to the right of target, so that the ball starts to the right. However, the closed clubface makes the ball hook back. Do the opposite for a slice. Align your body to the left of target, so that you swing left, but open the clubface by aiming the leading edge of the club at the actual target. The ball starts to the left, and slices back.

108. Studying how your arms recoil from the finish position can help you program a straight shot, slice and hook. On a straight shot, your arms recoil to a position in which your hands and the club shaft are centered on your chest, forming a letter Y. The position is symmetrical, and there's the same amount of bend in both wrists. 109. On a slice, the back of your left hand and forearm form an almost straight line, and there's more bend in the back of your right wrist. The Y points more to the right shoulder. 110. On a hook, the back of your right hand and forearm form almost a straight line and there's more bend in the back of your left wrist. The Y points more toward your left shoulder.

slide toward the toe. As a result, the ball starts a little to the right of the swing path. How much right, it is difficult to say—you just have to practice these shots to the point where you know.

Whether you fade the ball or slice it depends on how much you align your body to the left of target. If you align your body slightly to the left, you get a fade. The more you align your body left, the bigger the curve on the ball.

Suppose, however, that you do all this and instead of getting the fade or slice you expect, you pull the ball straight to the left. The reason is that you released your right hand too soon in the downswing, so that you squared the blade to the swing plane at impact instead of leaving it open.

To prevent this problem, firm up the pressure a little in your left hand at address and lighten the pressure in your right hand. Also, try to delay the release of the angles in your right arm and wrist. Your left hand then leads the clubhead into the shot more than usual, so that the clubface remains open.

When you hit a normal straight shot, study how your arms recoil from the finish position. They finish with your hands and the club shaft centered on the middle of your chest, the arms and shaft forming a perfect capital letter Y. If you've schooled yourself to keep your left wrist in the square position, then there's the same amount of bend in the back of each of your wrists. In all respects, the position of your hands, arms and club is perfectly symmetrical.

When you slice the ball, however, the picture changes. Because you've delayed the release of your right wrist and arm slightly, the back of your left hand and your forearm form an almost straight line and there's more bend in the back of your right wrist. Also the shaft is angled to your right as you face the hole in the finish. The Y formed by your arms and club shaft points closer to your right shoulder.

Once you have the feel of the "slice" finish versus the straight-ball finish, you can use this feel to preprogram a fade or slice as you prepare to hit the shot.

Another way of doing the same thing, which I like, is to imagine you're going to swing like a player who normally fades the ball. I use Lee Trevino's swing as my mental image. Trevino has to make a big effort to keep the clubface open at impact because of his strong grip. Bruce Lietzke and Craig Stadler also make good "fade" models. Faders are quicker, firmer hitters, have faster shoulder action, than hookers.

Club selection is obviously a major factor affecting fades and slices. With a driver through the 4-iron, a fade flies farther in the air than a straight ball; with a 5- through 7-iron, it flies the same distance; with the 8-iron through wedges, it flies shorter. The fade always tends to settle on the ground quickly. From about the 4-iron through the wedge, a fade will be about half a club weaker than a straight ball. The bigger the slice, the more club you'll need. For a moderate slice, you need about one club stronger; for a big "banana" ball, maybe three clubs stronger. You also can't expect to slice the ball much with any club more lofted than a 7-iron. With the short irons, the backspin you apply is stronger than the sidespin. If you need to curve the ball to the right, stick to the woods and the 1- through 7-irons.

DRAWS AND HOOKS

As you would expect, to make a ball curve to the left, the clubface must be closed to (aimed to the left of) the swing plane at impact. This puts the right-to-left spin on the ball.

To draw or hook the ball, you set up as though you were going to hit an imaginary target to the right of the actual target, your shoulders, hips and feet aligned right. Aim the leading edge of the blade at the actual target. In this way, the blade is closed in relation to the swing plane at impact, and you put right-to-left spin on the ball. With a draw or hook, the closed clubface traps the ball on the clubface so that the ball flies directly along the path of the swing through impact, before it curves to the left.

The degree of curve you put on the ball, again, depends on the amount you align your body to the right of target. A slight alignment of the body to the right results in a draw. The more you align to the right, the bigger the hook.

In the same way that allowing the clubface to close at impact wrecks a planned fade or slice, so keeping the face open through impact ruins a deliberate draw or hook. You can square the clubface to the swing plane at impact and push the ball straight to the right. To overcome this problem, lighten your grip slightly and swing freely. (Most hookers swing with big, relaxed swings. Examples: Tony Lema, Ben Crenshaw, Bobby Locke and Sam Snead.) You will then tend to release the angles in the right wrist and arm a little earlier through the hitting area, ensuring a closed blade and a released right side.

As with fade/slice shots, your recoil from the finish differs from that for a straight shot. Because you've speeded up the release of the angles in the right wrist and arm, your right wrist forms a straight line with the back of your right forearm, and your left wrist is bent more than on a straight shot. The club shaft is angled to the left in the finish. The Y formed by your arms and the club shaft points closer to your left shoulder.

Once you have the feel of this position, you can use it to program a hook or draw. Again, I think you'll find it useful to imagine yourself swinging like a player who draws the ball. My personal image is that of Tony Lema. Of today's golfers, I would suggest thinking of Gary Player's swing for a big hook, because Gary has to make such a big effort to close the blade at impact after opening it on the backswing. For a slight draw, visualize Gil Morgan's swing: he hits the ball dead flush, with just a little tail to the left at the finish of the ball's flight. He releases the right side very well, with no "Reverse C."

In selecting a club to draw or hook, remember that you're reducing the effective loft of the club. Make certain that the club you take has enough loft to get the ball into the air after you've closed it. A drawn or hooked ball will *always* roll farther than a straight ball, so use a weaker club than you usually would for the distance. With a driver through the wedges, the draw or hook flies shorter than a straight ball; from the 5-iron through the 7-iron, it flies about the same; from the 8-iron through wedges, it flies farther.

The only exception to this is a real "snap hook," which dives back to the ground so quickly it won't give you as much distance as normal except when the ground is hard. On such a shot, you may also have to make an effort to roll the right forearm over the left through impact to get the necessary spin.

Your lie affects your ability to hook or slice the ball. On a tight lie, it's easier to cut or fade the ball, because, to get down to the ball, you take a longer lead with your left hand through the ball, opening the blade at impact. The reverse happens when the ball is teed up: you tend to release your hands a little more and hook it. I'm not saying it's impossible to hook from a tight lie or fade it from a perched lie. (In fact, for a pro it's easy enough to hook the ball off a tight lie with a 5-iron through the wedges.) Certainly a tight lie favors a fade or slice, and a lie where the ball is up favors a draw or hook.

The type of ball you use also affects spin. For maximum sidespin and backspin, you have to use a ball with a balata cover.* This type of ball always has rubber windings around an inner core (wound ball). Most pros and good amateurs use it. At one time this was the only type of ball on the market. More recently, Du Pont came up with a material called Surlyn.® The chief advantage of balls with Surlyn covers is that they don't cut as easily. You can't put as much spin on a Surlyn ball—whether it's a wound ball or has a solid core (also known as a two-piece ball).

The good news with the Surlyn ball is that you don't hook and slice as much inadvertently; consequently you don't go into the woods so often. The bad news is that if you do go into the woods, you can't put a big hook or slice on the ball to curve it back to the green. A twenty-yard slice or hook with a balata ball translates into about a ten-yard slice or hook with a Surlyn ball.

What is true of sidespin is also true of backspin. You can't put so much backspin on a Surlyn ball that it sucks back. So, in a situation in which you need to stop the ball quickly, you can't just hit hard, as you would with a balata ball. With a Surlyn ball, you have to take one stronger club than usual and use the slow-motion swing I described earlier. Then the ball will drop softly on the green.

Regarding distance, take into account that Surlyn balls go at least one club, sometimes two clubs, farther than balata balls.

---

* Last year, I started playing with Spalding's new "Tour Edition"™ ball. This is a two-piece ball with a new cover material called Zinthane™ (not Surlyn). The ball's spin characteristics and performance are very close to that of a balata ball. However, unlike the balata ball, the new ball doesn't go out of round, is unaffected by temperature changes and lasts much longer. It's undoubtedly the ball of the future.

9

Trouble Shots

One of the best lessons of my life was when my father took me out to Harding Park one day with my clubs and a shag bag of balls and led me over to a stand of trees. We went deep into the woods, and there he dumped out the balls on the ground, saying, "Let's see what you can do from here."

At first I had all sorts of problems, and the balls were crashing into the branches. Eventually, I learned when and how to hit the ball high and low. On other occasions, my father had me practice from the rough, from hardpan and from uneven lies.

I recently took my son John, Jr., out and gave him the same experience. I highly recommend it. To paraphrase Clint Eastwood, "A golfer has to know his limitations." If you have practiced from all sorts of situations, then you know when you can go for it and when to chip back into play. You avoid the high numbers that wreck a round.

HIGH AND LOW SHOTS

To hit a high shot, play the ball a little farther forward in the stance. If you normally play an iron a couple of inches inside your left heel, play it off the left heel for a high shot. However, keep the blade square, unless you want to fade it, and your hands in their regular position opposite your left leg. This way, the grip end of the club is level with the clubhead, and it increases the effective loft of the club. You also should widen your stance a little by spreading your right foot a few inches farther to the right than usual. This puts your upper body more behind the ball, helping you get the ball up. Then go ahead and use your usual swing. Finish nice and high.

If you need to hit the ball extra high, then play the ball farther forward, off your left toe, and release the angles in your right wrist and arm earlier.

I should warn you that this technique works only if you have a good lie. Don't try to play the ball too far forward if it's on a bare lie or down in the grass. You'll merely thin it or hit it fat. In such circumstances, play the ball only an inch or so farther forward than usual, aim left, open the clubface,

111. One of the best lessons of my life was when my dad led me over to a stand of trees and said, "Let's see what you can do from here." Here I am giving my son John, Jr., the same type of lesson. I highly recommend it. You've got to know when you can go for a shot, and when to chip out safely.

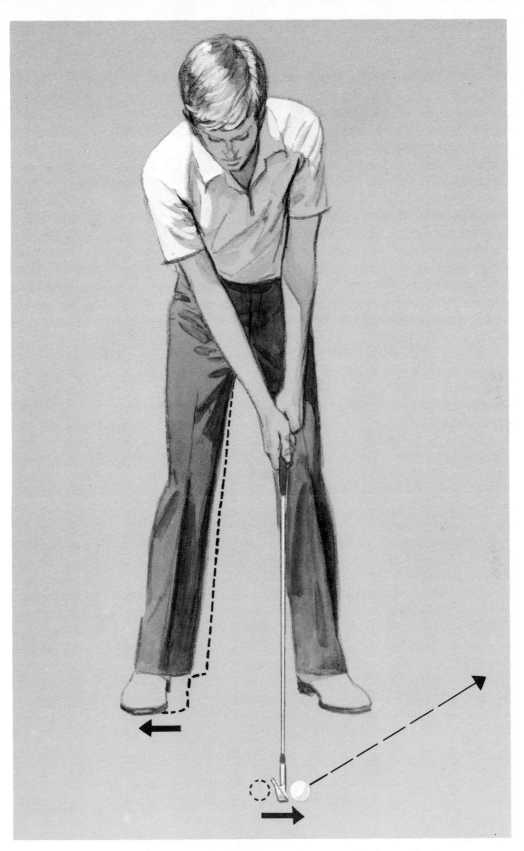

112. HIGH SHOT: Play the ball a little farther forward than usual. Also, widen your stance by spreading your right foot a few inches farther right than usual. This puts your upper body more behind the ball, helping you get the ball up.

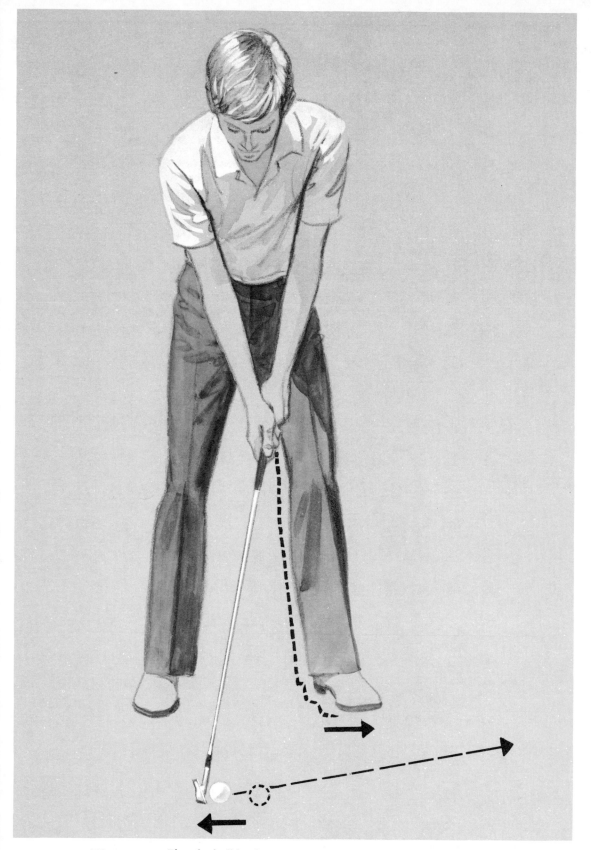

113. LOW SHOT: Play the ball back in your stance—the lower the shot you want the more you play it back. Also, widen your stance by spreading your left foot a few inches farther left than usual. This puts your upper body farther to the left than normal, helping you drive the ball down.

and use the fade/slice type of swing. In the downswing, hang back just a little on the right side.

To hit a low shot, move the ball back in your stance from its regular position. The lower you want to hit it, the more you move it back. As with the high shot, keep the blade square, but leave your hands in their regular position off the left leg. The grip end of the club is now tilted to your left in front of the clubhead, reducing the effective loft of the club (also called "hooding" the club). You should also widen your stance by spreading your left foot a few inches farther to the left than usual. This puts your upper body farther left than normal, helping you drive the ball down. Hold the club a bit more firmly with both hands to cut down on wrist action. Too much wrist action throws the ball up. In the downswing, make a conscious effort to shift the weight to the left side. Delay the release of the angles of the right wrist and arm by leading with your left hand through the ball. A good key is to think of finishing "low," with the club pointing at the hole in the follow-through.

Increasing or decreasing the effective loft of a club has a direct effect on your choice of club. Generally, a high shot with a particular club will fly as far but not roll as much as a normal shot. A low shot will come to earth sooner, but usually will have more roll. On low shots, be careful that the club you select has enough loft after you've hooded it. Don't take a long iron and play the ball back opposite your right foot. All you'll do is rip the ball along the ground and scare the worms.

ODD LIES

When your ball goes into the rough, the first thing you should look at is the lie. You have to study not only the length of grass, but how the ball is lying in it: whether it is perched, on the ground or somewhere in between. Your ball can also come to rest on hardpan or against a tree. Each one of these circumstances can dictate a different type of shot or club selection.

When your ball lies in light rough, say up to about two inches in height, there's usually no need to change your technique. However, your choice of club will vary. If the ball is lying normally just off the ground, you can count on an extra five yards of roll and possibly a flier which goes approximately twenty yards farther than from a normal fairway lie with a 4-iron to a wedge. This is because you can't pinch the ball between the club and ground at impact as you normally could from the fairway. If you take your normal club for the distance and the shot "flies" on you, you can go twenty yards over the green. Play this shot with a weaker club than normal. If it "flies," you'll be on the green. If it doesn't, at least you'll be in front of the green with an easy pitch or chip for your par.

I should add here that you can get "fliers" from the fairway, too. If your ball lies in clover, you'll almost certainly get one. You should also look out for fairways where the grass is longer than usual or is wet. In all the cases I've described, the flier comes from clover, grass or water getting in between the clubface and the ball at impact. They lubricate the clubface so that it can't grip the ball as it usually does.

If your ball is perched—sitting up on top of the grass—then you should modify your technique. Play the shot much as you would a fairway bunker. Choke down on the club a little so that you can get the clubhead to the level of the ball. Stand slightly more erect than usual. Now swing very smoothly, striking the ball with a "sweeping" type of action. Don't hit down on a perched ball—you could go right underneath it.

If your ball lies in heavy rough, the first thing to do is to play the ball back in your stance. The heavier the rough is, the more you must play it back. With the ball back, you will bring the club up sharply on the backswing and come down on the ball steeply. In this way, you should avoid plowing through the grass in back of the ball, slowing the clubhead. A good key is to imagine that you're going to hit something very heavy—a bag of sand, for example. This gears up your muscles to really hit down on the ball.

For extra distance out of the rough, align your shoulders, hips and feet to an imaginary target ten yards right of your actual target. Close the clubface by aiming the leading edge of the club at the actual target.

The swing you use is a pull/hook. In other words, you swing back on the plane established by your body at address, but you deliberately come over the top of the ball with your right shoulder so that you swing through the ball on line to your actual target. Your downswing plane is tilted to the left of the plane you swung back on. This shot should be used when you can let the ball run. Don't try it when you must carry a bunker or water hazard.

As in baseball, this pulled shot is a very strong shot. Also, even though you've closed the blade, you won't hook the ball much to the left of target, because it's hard to put sidespin on the ball from heavy rough. The ball will roll strongly once it strikes the ground.

Closing the blade has another purpose: a cleaner hit. A closed blade ensures that the toe of the club cuts through the grass first, whereas if you open the blade, as is commonly taught, the grass grabs the heel of the club, closing it viciously. You smother the ball, and it stays in the rough.

Regarding club selection, playing the ball back in your stance and closing the clubface effectively reduces the loft on the club. So, never use a long iron on this shot. I seldom use anything less lofted than a 5-iron. From heavy rough, use a 7-, 8- or 9-iron or a wedge. However, if you want to play a rough shot with a 5-wood, or a 7-wood, that's fine, but not from rough deeper than about four inches.

If your ball comes to rest on hardpan, the easiest way to get the ball up is to put a little fade on the ball. Aim the leading edge of the club at the target, take a slightly open stance and play the ball a little back in the stance to ensure that you catch the ball cleanly. The slightly firmer left-hand grip you use on this shot helps prevent the club twisting on contact. While the fade swing gives you a slightly steeper angle of descent on the ball, it also helps you get it up in the air.

If your ball comes to rest near trees, then usually the low or high shots I've previously described will do the trick. However, sometimes your ball is so close to a tree that you can't take a regular right-handed shot. I had this experience recently playing in the Benson & Hedges Tournament, in England. My ball was on a semi-bare lie right next to a tree and I had no swing —right-handed. Even worse, I had a grove of trees in front of me, and I could see only a small opening in them to the green. It was a desperate situation, because I was in danger of missing the cut. Now, I have a Tommy Armour blade putter. It has a concave back with about the loft of a 6-iron. I swung the putter left-handed. The ball came flying out just like a 6-iron, landed inches from the hole and even sucked back five feet.

The backs of Ping putters have big hitting surfaces and are easy to hit. However, if you don't have a putter that allows you to hit the ball left-handed, then there are alternatives.

Probably the easiest is to stand with your back to the hole, your feet a little apart, and the ball to the right of your right foot. Grip a short iron at the bottom of the handle with just your right hand, aiming the leading edge at the target, and punch the ball behind you with a firm right wrist and arm. If you practice the shot, you'll find that you can put some wrist into it after a while. This will give you more distance.

The other shot definitely requires practice. Turn the clubhead of a wedge upside down so that the blade faces the hole when you take the left-handed stance. Then swing. When you hit left-handed, remember to reverse all the normal fundamentals: grip with the left hand below the right, keep your right arm extended and your left relatively "soft," and so on.

HILLY LIES

There are four types of hilly lie: uphill, downhill, ball above feet and ball below feet. In each case, you must adjust your stance and swing to the slope. There are a couple of points that apply to all of them. First, I don't normally recommend practice swings, but I do on tough lies like these. A couple of practice swings taken from the same type of lie you have to play can give you a good idea of how much adjustment you must make. Second, these lies force you to address the ball and swing from an unfamiliar position. If you try to hit the ball hard, you tend to lose your balance and it ruins the shot. Instead, shorten your swing a little and swing smoothly. Take a stronger club (for example, a 4-iron instead of a 5-iron) on all but downhill lies.

Uphill. When you have a mild uphill lie, with your left foot one or two inches higher than your right, the most important point is that the club must swing through the ball on a path that parallels the slope as closely as possible. To do this, you have to tilt your body to the right at address so that it is at right angles to the slope. This will put more weight on your right foot than usual. A good key is to think of your left shoulder—position it a little higher than normal—and you'll get the right setup. Because this position increases the effective loft of a club, use one less lofted club than you normally would. Play for a ten-yard hook.

These adjustments work fine on a slightly uphill lie, but if the slope is severe, you'll find it impossible to tilt your body so that it is at right angles to the slope. You won't be able to keep your balance—there's too much weight on your right foot. Then, you have to allow your body to be more vertical by allowing your left leg to bend more than usual.

On a steep uphill lie, try to set your weight about 40 percent on your left leg, 60 percent on your right. Anchor your feet and legs and use almost no weight shift going back. Play the shot mostly with your hands and arms. Take two or three clubs stronger than usual to make up for the loss in power.

With the more lofted clubs—say the 5-iron through wedges—set up as close to 50–50 as possible and hit straight into the hill. The ball does fly lower, but you have more control, with only about ten yards hook. I must admit, though, that this is tough on the wrists. You can't, of course, hit into the hill with clubs like the 3-wood or 3-iron, because you'll drive the ball into the ground.

On an uphill lie, most people draw or hook the ball, depending on the severity of the slope, the reason being that when you set up with more weight on your right foot than your left at address, it becomes impossible to shift your weight back to your left foot in the downswing as you normally would. You hit more with your hands and arms, closing the blade. Even with a 50–50 setup on severe slopes, your legs are pretty much anchored. Again, you're forced to hit mainly with the hands and arms.

Downhill. On a moderate downhill lie, where your left foot is slightly lower than your right, reverse the adjustments for the uphill lie. Play the ball back in the stance and tilt your shoulder down so that it is level with the ground contour. This way, you can swing through parallel to the slope. Since this lie reduces the effective loft of the club, the ball flies lower, with a lot of roll. Therefore, you need a more lofted club than usual.

On a severe downhill lie, you're going to find it impossible to keep your balance at address without bending your right leg more than usual. To catch the ball cleanly, play the ball way back in your stance, from the middle of the stance to just inside the right foot.

On a downhill lie, it's tough to stop your upper body from going down the slope with your lower body in the downswing. As a result, your body gets

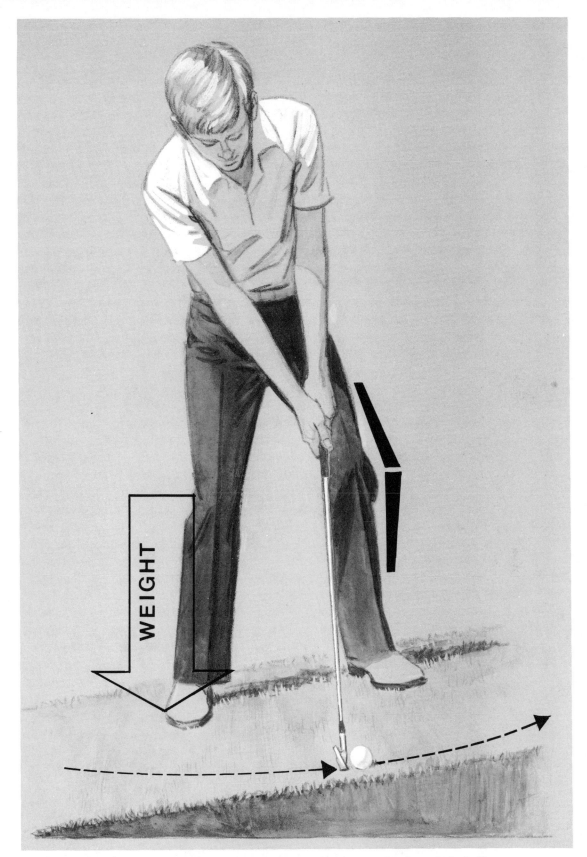

114. UPHILL LIE: Put more weight on your right foot so that you can hit through the ball on a path that parallels the slope. On more severe lies, bend your left knee more than usual. Allow for a little hook.

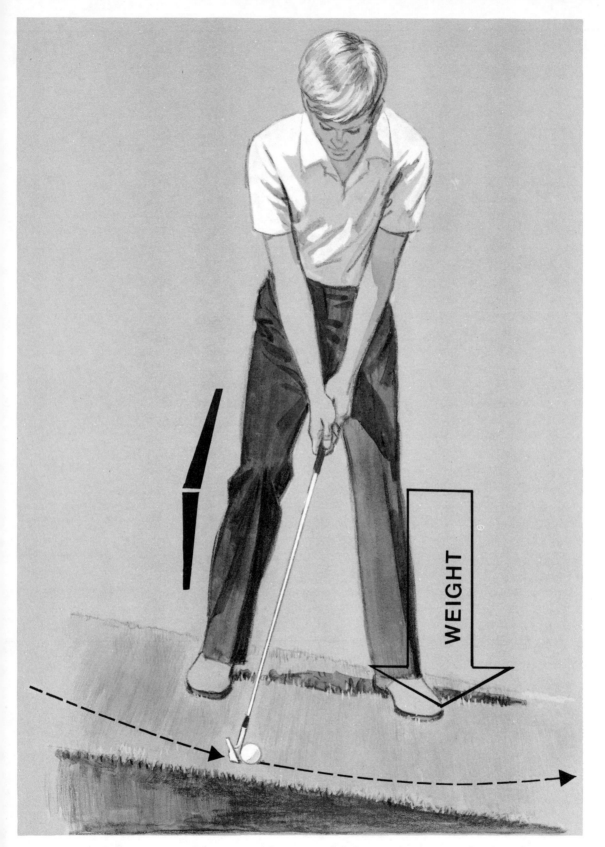

115. DOWNHILL LIE: Put more weight on your left foot so that you can hit through on a path that parallels the slope. On more severe lies, bend your right knee more than usual. Allow for a pushed slice.

116. BALL ABOVE FEET: Stand more erect and farther from the ball than usual. Choke down a little on the club. Allow for a hook.

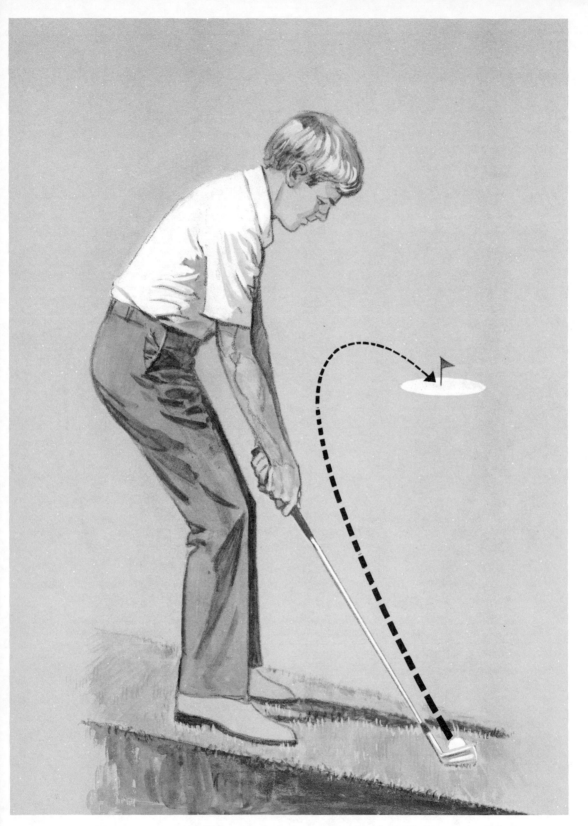

117. BALL BELOW FEET: Use a "sit down" posture, with the ball closer to you than usual. Hold the club at the end of the grip. Allow for a push/fade.

ahead of your hands, leaving the blade open at impact. Compensate for the slice or push by aiming a little to the left of target.

You can't, of course, compensate for the slice by closing the clubface, because in most cases this reduces the loft on the club to the point where the ball won't get up in the air. If anything, do the opposite. Play for a fade or slice, depending on the severity of the downhill lie. Say you have a situation in which you want to hit a fairway wood—say on your second shot to a par 5 —and you have a slight downhill lie. If you open your stance and fade the ball a little, the fade helps you get the ball up. However, don't try to hit a 3-wood or a 1- or 2-iron off these lies.

Ball Above Feet. Most golfers know that you hook from a ball-above-feet lie, but don't understand why. The most severe ball-above-feet lie possible would be if the ball were up in a bush, tree or cliff at chest level. From this type of lie, the clubface rotates open to closed violently, causing a big hook. Obviously, the less severe the slope, the less hook you get. Aim twenty yards or more to the right to allow for the hook.

When you address the ball lying on a moderate ball-above-feet lie, it's natural to stand a little more erect than usual. You have less flex in your knees and stand farther from the ball than usual. If you made no adjustments, you would swing on a very flat plane. However, if you choke down on the club a little, it gives you more control and gets you closer to the ball. You will many times pull/hook this shot, because your body moves down the slope. Try to finish with your hands high.

On a severe ball-above-feet lie, you have to choke down even more. You'll also find that it's very difficult to turn the body a lot without losing balance. This means that you have to play the shot more with your hands and arms, a distinct power loss. Your priority should be to try to hit the ball solid and not whiff it. Depending on the severity of the slope, you may have to take two or three clubs more than usual.

When you've practiced the shot sufficiently, experiment with opening the blade at address before you take your regular grip. A ten-yard slice swing will fly about straight. It's a good way to offset the hook.

Ball Below Feet. To hit a ball below your feet, the key thought is to "get down" to the slope with your butt and knees. Get into a bent-kneed, "sit down" position. Play the ball closer to your feet than usual, holding your club at the end of the grip.

Be very careful not to lose your balance in the downswing, "falling" down the slope into the ball. Then you push the ball, slice it or even shank it (the ball is struck by the hosel of the club, flying viciously to the right).

You can't get much power with the ball below your feet. So take more club.

Don't use much body action. Brace the body and swing mainly with the hands and arms.

On severe slopes, you'll find that your body turn is very limited. The power loss translates into your needing a much stronger club than usual. You'll also find that you tend to "come over the top" on the downswing and top the ball. This is one shot in which you must stay down and try to hit the ball flush.

From all of these awkward stances, the golfer that uses a lot of body in the swing is really at a disadvantage. Golfers that can pretty much immobilize the body, get comfortable, and then use their hands and arms, rather than the body, play these shots the best.

The main thing is to get some experience with all these lies. Then you can experiment with trying to cut down the amount of slice or hook. The big thing is knowing what to expect and play for it.

I've just given you what I call the "textbook" tendencies from these lies and what you do to allow for them or minimize them. However, everyone's swing is a little different and so the effect of these lies can vary from player to player.

In my own game I know that when I play a shot from a ball-below-feet lie, I tend to come over the top and pull the ball a little. I don't do what you're supposed to do: push/fade the ball. If I kept aiming left "to allow for the slice," I would easily be fouled up. I'm tall with short arms—everyone is different.

That is why it's so important that you get out and practice from these lies. You can then see how they affect *your* swing and *your* shots!

10

The Short Game

In the long game, I explained the basic golf swing, and later the modifications that produced the various shots. I'm going to follow the same plan for the short game. I'll start with the basic pitch shot, then cover the variations, before going to the very short shots around the green, called chip shots.

PITCH SHOTS

The pitch is just a miniature version of the short-iron swing I described earlier. The same fundamentals apply: the weaker grip, the early set, a firm, descending blow to set up a lowish trajectory with plenty of spin, the very firm left wrist through impact, the circular arc and so forth. The only differences are that you're playing the shot with a wedge and you're not making a full swing. Depending on the distance, you use a quarter-, half- or three-quarter swing.

As a rule, swing through the ball almost the same amount as you swing back. On a quarter swing, you'd swing back to a point where your hands are just to the right of your right leg, then through to a point just to the left of your left leg. On a half swing, you'd swing your hands back to waist height and through to waist height. On a three-quarter swing, you'd swing back to shoulder height and through to shoulder height. Even though the pitch is on a smaller scale than a full shot, it still should be a free-flowing back-and-forth movement.

One point I'd like to emphasize is that there is no need to *think* of hitting down on the ball. You take care of that at address. In exactly the same manner as you narrowed the width of your stance from the driver down to the full wedge shot, you now narrow your stance gradually as you get nearer the green, and use shorter swings so that you swing up and down in a steeper arc. You also have progressively moved the ball back in your stance, so that on a normal wedge shot, the ball is opposite your left ear. Your weight is 60 percent on your left foot. These adjustments also set up a crisp,

118–121. The pitch is just a miniature of the short-iron swing—the ball back in the stance, about opposite the left side of your neck, the weaker grip, the early set, and a firm, descending blow to set up a low trajectory with plenty of spin, your left wrist firm through impact, the circular arc. The only difference is that you're not using a full swing. As a general rule, swing through the ball the same amount you swing back.

slightly descending blow. You should take a very shallow divot, almost brushing the grass roots. Don't dig deep divots.

It's very helpful on these shorter shots to set up with a slightly open stance. With your hips set a little open and your shoulders square, this helps create a little more torque between your upper body and your right leg going back, making it easier to start down with your knees and get through the ball.

In a pitch shot, let your knees provide the rhythm. In sizing up a pitch shot, try to visualize how hard it would be to throw the ball underhand at the green. In a throw you use your knees a lot. You should do the same in the pitch shot, rather like the knee action in bowling. Don't stand there stiff-legged—you'll have no touch at all.

Because the normal pitch shot should be a slower, shorter swing than the

full swing, there's a tendency to get "lazy" through impact. It's all too easy to "scoop" the ball up with your right hand. This breaks down your straight left wrist, so that a bigger angle appears in the back of your wrist. As a result, the clubhead gets ahead of the hands, increasing the effective loft on the club. Because you use more loft than you intend, the ball always flies too high and finishes short of the target. For a firm, solid hit, you want a very, very firm left wrist at impact and for a few inches after impact.

The clubs one uses in pitch shots are very important. Too many juniors think that the pitching wedge is just for pitching, and the sand wedge just for sand shots. Instead, think of them as short irons with different lofts. Study the shot at hand and use the wedge that will most easily give you the result you want. For example, if you need extra loft on a pitch, there's no point in opening the blade of a pitching wedge if you could get the same result by playing a straightforward pitch with the more lofted sand wedge. You do need to establish your own safe maximum distance with the sand wedge. When you try to use the sand wedge for too long a shot, the ball flies too high, with a bad, "rainbow" flight and with no spin. Find the maximum distance where you still get the proper ball flight and spin, and use the sand

122–123. The knees provide the rhythm in a pitch shot and much of the feel for distance. When sizing up a pitch, I try to visualize how hard I'd throw the ball underhanded. You should do the same.

wedge only for shots within this range. Use a pitching wedge otherwise. Many pros now use a third, very lofted (about 60 degrees) sand wedge for short pitch and sand shots.

When you use a sand wedge from grass, you have to be aware of the "bounce" on the club. The bounce is the degree to which the back edge of the flange is lower than the leading edge when the club is soled squarely at address.

If your sand wedge has little or no bounce, then you can play most pitch shots normally. However, the more bounce it has, the more you have to guard against skulling the ball (hitting it at the equator) off a tight lie. You have to take bounce off the club by playing the ball back in your stance and hitting down on the ball, rather than sweeping it. This results in a lower shot. Be careful about opening the clubface, because this creates extra bounce. From a good lie, you usually can get away with it, but from a poor lie, it's easy to skull the ball. If you have to open the clubface from a poor lie, and doubt whether you can slip your sand wedge under the ball, use your pitching wedge instead.

When you're a beginner, the easiest way to obtain different distances with the wedge is to vary the length of your swing and the amount you choke down on the club. On a longer pitch, you might choke down an inch or so and use a three-quarter swing. On a short pitch, you might choke down a couple of inches and use a quarter swing. After a while, you can be more subtle. You fine-tune the distance by swinging a little harder or more softly.

All the techniques I described in shot making can be used in the short game. If you want a shot with a lot of spin, use a short, brisk, firm-wristed swing. If you want to drop the ball on the green (say, if it's hard), then use a long, slow swing. If you need a high shot, play the ball forward a little. If you need a low shot, play it back. You also can use slice and hook spin to work the ball into a pin tucked behind a bunker. With the loft on wedges, the ball won't curve much in the air, but the spin does take effect when the ball hits the ground, kicking the ball in to the left or right slightly.

One thing I strongly suggest is to experiment with your wedges. They're the most versatile clubs in your bag. You're going to encounter all sorts of lies and situations in the short game. You need to be ready to cope with them.

If you have a perched lie, with the ball sitting on top of the grass, sole the club even with the ball and use a more sweeping type of shot. Tee up with the ball opposite your left ear, the blade squarely at the hole, your stance slightly open. Then take a firm grip so that you swing the club with your arms and with practically no wrist in the stroke. This shot doesn't have the backspin of a regular pitch. If you need more stop, play the ball a little forward in the stance.

If you're playing from hardpan, position the ball opposite your left ear. Then open the blade of the wedge a little to ensure that the blade skids through even if you hit the ball a little fat. If you play the shot with a square blade, the clubhead can stick in the hardpan.

In the rough, play the ball back in your stance, under your nose. You can then pick the club up quickly and descend sharply on the ball. If the grass is so thick that you can't put the club cleanly on the ball, then play the shot in just the same way you'd play a regular sand shot. Set up with open shoulders and feet, positioning the ball one inch inside your left heel. Set the blade at the target or slightly right of it if you need more height to stop the ball. Take a relatively firm grip so that you can cut down through the grass behind the ball. Then use an early set, swinging the club back and through along the path established by the shoulders, from out to in. Swing the club with the same strength you would use on a bunker shot of similar length. Pretend you are in a trap.

When using a Surlyn ball, you will find that it doesn't take spin like a balata ball. If you have a short pitch over a bunker to a tight pin placement, it's no good using a faster swing to get backspin—the ball will run about twice as much when it hits the green, rather than stopping after the first bounce. Instead, use a variation of the slow swing shot. I call it the "telephone booth" shot, because you use such a narrow swing.

Open the blade of your wedge and grip your club very lightly for maximum wrist action. Play the ball a little forward in your stance off your left heel, with your hands over the ball. Then take a very slow swing, setting the club early and allowing your right elbow to fold sooner than usual. Then hit down on the ball. After impact, the club should come up quickly with your left wrist cupping sooner in the follow-through than in any other shot. As a result, the ball is flipped high in the air and drops softly on the green.

If the green is very hard, address the ball slightly off the toe; a toe hit absorbs energy and the ball drops even deader on the green.

CHIPPING

I used a conventional stroke in chipping for years. I set up with a narrow, slightly open stance, the ball off my left heel, and choked down on the club so that only an inch or so of grip showed below my right forefinger. I had the handle of my club level with the front of the ball, with my left arm and club shaft forming a straight line. As I chipped the ball, I keyed on maintaining that straight line. This produced a firm, consistent stroke with little wristiness, much like putting.

From a good lie, you'll find that this simple, sweeping stroke is very effective. However, if the lie is bad, you have to play the ball back in the stance.

124. In the conventional chipping stroke, you choke down on the club, ball about off the left heel, and key on keeping your left arm and the club shaft in a straight line. This produces a firm, consistent stroke with little wristiness.

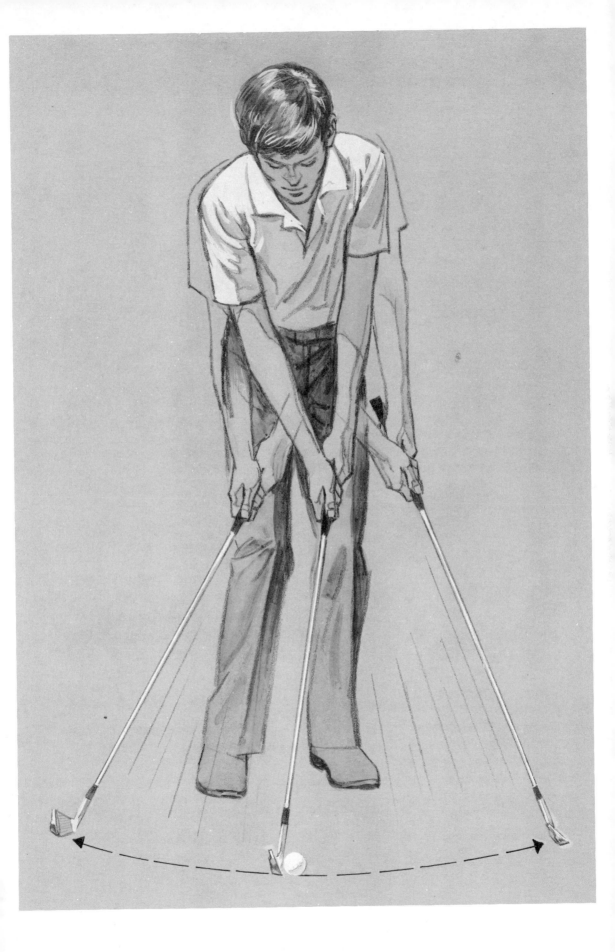

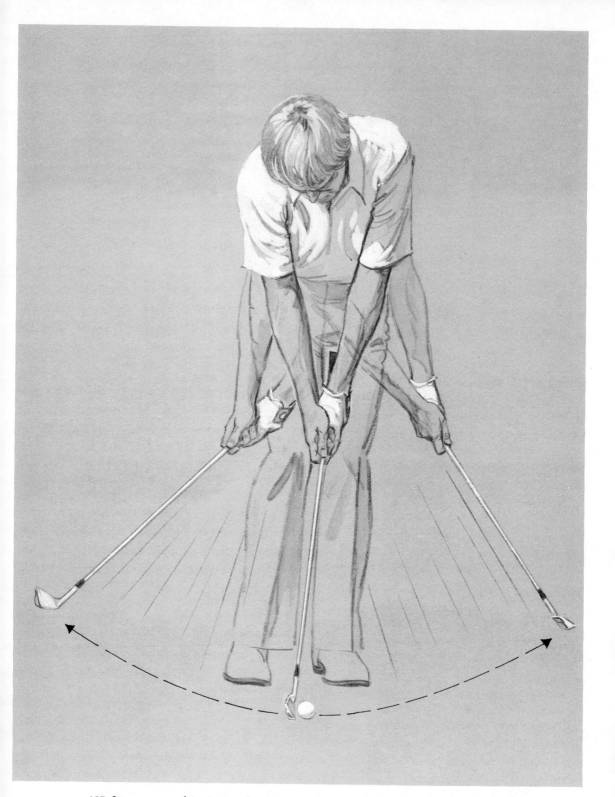

125. I now use a chipping stroke as close to my putting stroke as is practical. I use the reverse overlap, choke down to the length of my putter, and bring the ball in about four inches from a line across my toes. I take the club back and through with my arms.

I'm mentioning the conventional stroke because you may try it and like it. However, I must admit I no longer use it myself. I went to a new method of chipping in 1983. You can't believe how much it has helped me. I've gone from being a mediocre chipper to a good one by Tour pro standards.

I now use a chipping stroke that is as close to my putting stroke as is practical.

I use my putting grip, the reverse overlap, with my left index finger running down the last three fingers of my right hand. I bend forward a lot from the waist so that I choke down on the club to the length of my putter. With my hands in their regular position off the left thigh, I play the ball for a normal lie about an inch inside my right foot. I also bring the club in toward my body as close as I can and still be comfortable. In my case, that is about four inches away from a line across my toes. I use a slightly open stance, with my feet a few inches apart. My weight is fairly even or slightly on my left foot.

To accommodate this position, the heel of the club is slightly in the air. Also, my hands are arched downward, which cuts down on wristiness.

In the stroke, I take the club back and through with my arms, with practically no wrist, and no legs. I pretend that I'm putting, and this gives me a feel for how hard to hit. I find I can use this method up to about a hundred feet.

This type of stroke has several advantages over the conventional stroke. First, with the club so close to my body, my arms are better connected to my body, so that the shoulders work automatically. In the conventional stroke, the arms can work independently, taking the club inside of the proper path. Second, the club goes almost straight back along the target line and straight through, which is far more dependable than the conventional stroke, in which the club goes back more to the inside, then comes through the ball from the inside to square and back to the inside. Third, the clubface stays squarer to the target line through the stroke, rather than opening and closing.

Besides this method, the other thing that has helped my chipping more than anything else is never soling the club firmly on the ground. I just sole the club enough so that the clubhead sits level with the ball. You just pick the ball off. It really helps, because whatever the lie is, you don't have to contend with the grass roots, just the top part of the grass blades.

I do vary my ball position, though. For a slightly higher shot, I move the ball a little more toward my left foot. On a mediocre lie, I play the ball back off my right foot, or even to the right of the foot if the lie is really bad—say the ball's lying in a divot or there's a clump of grass behind the ball.

Whichever method you use, there are several points that apply to both:

I think you should swing back and through at a constant speed. If you swing back at one speed and slow down through the ball, it becomes extremely difficult to judge distance. If you accelerate through the ball, you're halfway toward jerking the stroke, or "popping it," as it is called.

The constant speed will vary from person to person. If you have a long, smooth, full swing, then you should have a long, smooth stroke. Ben Crenshaw's tempo comes to mind. If you normally swing faster, then Tom Watson or Lanny Wadkins would be a good model.

In selecting a club, pick the least lofted club that will land the ball at least a yard onto the green. You never want to land the ball in the fringe, unless you have to, because the bounce and roll of the ball is less consistent. With my method, of course, you have to select a more lofted club for any given chip than with the conventional method. This is because, with the hands ahead of the clubhead, you deloft the club to some extent.

Regarding which clubs you should use, I think it's necessary to learn how to chip with every club to learn which ones give you your best results. With my method, you can use any club, but always use the least lofted club possible. It's easier to hit less lofted clubs solidly.

One last word about the type of ball you're using. Surlyn balls come off the clubface a little faster than balata, and roll a little farther. If you switch from one type of ball to the other, practice your chips with the ball you're going to use. This way, you adjust your touch to the new ball.

A lot of youngsters ask me, "Johnny, I hit my pitches and chips solidly, but how do I develop touch?" There's just one answer to that question and that is practice. The hardest thing about the short game is that each shot is a different distance, and each swing has to be a little longer or shorter. You have to get to the point where you can look at a shot and *know* what swing will do the job.

To make such practice fun, there's nothing better than going out on an evening and competing against someone else—see who can get the ball closest to the hole on the practice green, or who can sink the most. Choose all sorts of lies and distances. Always have a small bet going, even if it's just a soft drink or play money for the winner. Win or lose, your short game is bound to improve.

If you have a good short game, you can score decently even on the days you aren't hitting the full shots well or in bad weather.

The golfer with the good short game is always consistent and always has the advantage!

11

Sand Play

When I was a junior golfer, between the ages of twelve and seventeen, I probably hit more sand shots than any other shot besides putting. My father taught me the basic techniques of sand play, and a good friend of mine, Ronald O'Connor, who literally loved sand play, supplied me with companionship and competition.

I grew up playing golf at the Olympic Club, in San Francisco. On the club's Ocean course, there was a little practice bunker by the driving range. It was really deep, the green elevated as high as your head. Because it was difficult to get out of, Ron and I used to have it all to ourselves to practice in. He would sometimes hit five hundred sand shots a day, and he completely wore out his sand wedge during those years. I didn't hit quite as many as he, but I was close.

We would invent all sorts of games in the sand. We got a big kick out of seeing how much we could make a ball back up or spin sideways. To this day, I remember how I once backed a ball up sixty feet on a flat green.

Sand play was fun for me as a kid, as it should be for you. Ron and I looked at each shot as a challenge and were disappointed when we failed to get the ball within five feet of the hole. We took pride in our developing skills and never left the bunker until we'd each holed out several shots.

As a beginner, you should have the same attitude toward sand play. If you think of sand play as "play in sand," then you'll enjoy learning the shots and improving your skills through constant practice.

THE SKID SHOT

As a starting point, let's explore the "skid" shot, the standard "explosion" shot you play from a good lie in a bunker close to the green.

On any sand shot, the first essential is to dig in well about one or two inches with both feet until you're solidly planted. This prevents your sliding around during the swing. Although you can't touch the sand with your club

126. On any sand shot, dig in well with your feet to prevent slipping. Open the sand wedge so that its leading edge is aimed slightly right of target. Open the stance so that the shoulders and feet are aligned slightly left of target.

without incurring a penalty, you can get a good idea of the sand's texture through your feet.

The second essential is to open the clubface so that the leading edge is aimed slightly (about five feet) to the right of target. Opening the clubface brings the flange on the sand wedge into play. A good sand wedge always has some "bounce" on it. (Bounce is the degree to which the back edge of the flange is lower than the leading edge when the club is soled squarely at address.) By opening the clubface, you increase the bounce, so that the sand wedge skids through the sand, rather than digging in.

Having opened the clubface, take a normal grip and open your stance, so that your shoulders and feet are aligned five feet to the left of target. Play the ball about one inch inside of your left heel, aiming to hit the sand about two inches behind the ball with the leading edge of the sand wedge.

The swing is similar to the short-iron swing described earlier, including the early set of the club and descending blow with a firm left wrist. The difference is that you swing the club up and down the path established by your open shoulders, from out to in—you're swinging to a target five feet left of the hole. The open clubface will compensate for this, and the ball should fly straight on a line about halfway between the line of your swing and the line of clubface aim. As you would expect, such a swing puts a lot of slice spin on the ball, and the ball kicks slightly right on landing. You must allow for this by aiming to land the ball on a spot a little to the left of the hole.

It's very important to keep the clubface open through the ball. If you roll your wrists to the left, the clubface will close and you'll dig into the sand too deeply. To avoid this, use the same technique you did on the deliberate slice: firm up the grip with your left hand. Also delay the release of the angles in your right wrist and arm in the downswing. It's a very crisp swing—imagine you are Tom Watson. My father used to tell me to imagine that I had a glass balanced on the clubface. The only way the glass could stay there was if the clubface remained open through impact.

Here's one of the commonest faults in playing the skid shot. When you address the ball, you should hold the club above the point where you intend to enter the sand. Now, in the takeaway, what a lot of beginners do is take the club *down* and away low as they would for a normal long swing. The club goes *down* and away before going up. This puts the low point of the swing behind the intended point of entry. They then either hit much too far behind the ball or catch the ball after the low point in the swing arc, when the club is rising, and skull the shot. To avoid this error, concentrate on the early set, breaking the wrists immediately in the takeaway.

To vary the distance you get with the skid shot, you basically vary the length and speed of your swing and the alignment of your body and the clubface. Varying the length and speed of your swing we've covered before, but it is very important. Varying alignment deserves a bit more discussion.

The basic rule is, the shorter the shot the more you align the body to the left of target and aim the clubface to the right, opening the clubface. The more you open the clubface the more you increase the effective loft of the club and the higher and shorter the ball flies. Also, the more you open the clubface the more slice spin you put on the ball.

As you go toward longer shots, the less you align the body to the left and the clubface to the right. With a less open clubface, the ball flies lower and farther, with less slice spin.

The important thing to remember is that the degree to which you align your body left and aim the clubface right should always match. If you set your body to swing toward a point ten feet left of target, set the clubface at a point ten feet right of target. Then the open stance and open blade offset each other and the ball flies straight between the line of swing and clubface aim.

I pointed out earlier that you could use the basic skid shot technique out of heavy rough. Everything I've said so far applies when you play the shot outside the bunker, except for "digging in," of course. Actually, the skid shot is one of the handiest shots you'll ever learn. It's such a safe shot, especially if you have any misgivings about your lie.

I don't believe in the old-fashioned theory that on an explosion shot you should use the same length of swing and vary distance by the amount you hit behind the ball. If you hit too far behind the ball, you never put any backspin on it, and you'll have trouble when the greens are fast or you're playing to a green sloping away from you. If you hit very close to the ball, you get a tremendous amount of backspin and sidespin, more than on any other shot, because the thin layer of sand between the clubface and the ball at impact acts like an abrasive. This is a dangerous shot—you obviously run the risk of skulling the ball. In special situations, such as when the green slopes from right to left, it can be useful, but if the green slopes from left to right, you obviously need a softer shot, one with less sidespin so it doesn't spin down the slope.

The ideal normal skid shot is one that gives you a margin for error. It's a neutral shot, in between these two extremes, with a little bit of backspin and sidespin. This way, if you hit the ball a little too fat, instead of the ball landing, say, ten feet from the hole, it lands fifteen feet from the hole and rolls up close. If you hit the ball a little thin, it lands five feet from the hole, has a tremendous amount of spin and still finishes stiff.

I told you before to hit about two inches behind the ball. That's just a starting point. You should find your own best distance to hit behind the ball by studying how your ball reacts when it lands on the green. If your ball lands and starts rolling forward right away, you're hitting too far behind the ball. If you always get an enormous amount of backspin and sidespin, you're hitting too close to the ball, at least for a standard skid shot. What you're looking for is the ball that lands, checks and then trickles. That's your happy medium.

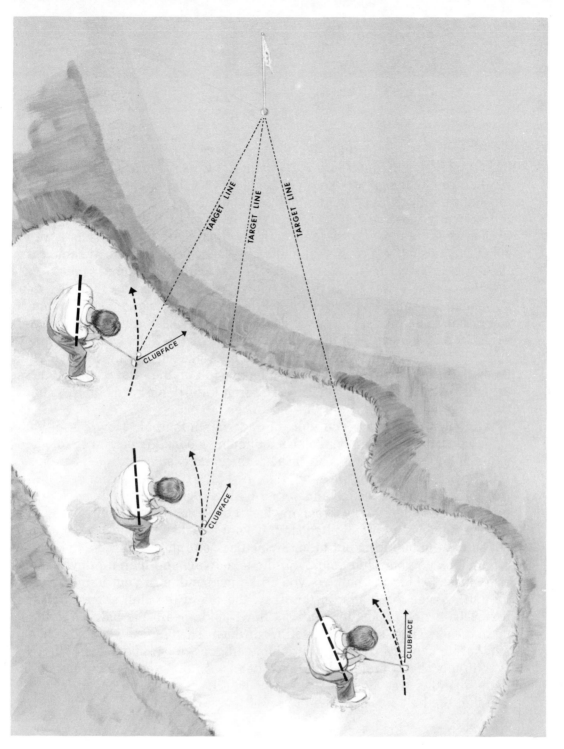

127. To vary the distance of a sand shot, you vary the length and speed of your swing and the alignment of your body and the clubface. The shorter the shot the more you open the clubface and stance. As you go toward longer shots, the less you open the clubface and stance. The degree to which you open the clubface and stance should always match. Then the open clubface and stance offset each other, and the ball flies midway between the line of swing and clubface aim.

SPECIAL SHOTS

If the sand is firmer than usual, then a very good shot to play is one I picked up from watching Gary Player and Chi Chi Rodriguez, two of the best sand players in the game. What you do is play the ball back in the middle of the stance with an open blade, pick the club up very quickly and hit down firmly, really close to the ball. The ball comes out lower than usual, but because you hit close to the ball with an open blade, the shot has a lot of spin. The ball takes a long skid and stops super fast. It's a good shot when the pin is just over a mound or at the top level of a two-tiered green.

If the sand is very hard or packed down tightly because of rain, use your normal skid technique, but don't open the face of your sand wedge as much as normal. With too open a clubface, the club bounces off the sand and you skull the ball. Instead, just open the clubface *slightly*. Then key on making a good, crisp "down" motion through the ball. Make sure you get underneath the ball. Because you're putting less effective loft on the sand wedge—you're using maybe 11-iron loft, rather than 13-iron loft—don't swing quite as hard as you normally would from that distance.

With most sand irons, you will get underneath the ball. However, if your sand wedge has a huge bounce, use a pitching wedge. Its narrower sole and minimal bounce will let it skid through the sand easily.

If the ball is buried in the sand, I use a shot that's unusual but very effective. I take my sand wedge and set up with a slightly open stance, with the ball positioned midway between my feet. I open my blade slightly. My backswing resembles a normal pitch shot. It's not like the skid shot, in which you cut across the ball from out to in. Swing back and through on the line to the target. Pick up your club quickly in the takeaway, and then hit down about two inches behind the ball. As you strike the sand, turn your hands over to the left, closing the blade. In this way, the toe of the club enters the sand first. This action makes the club cut down underneath the ball, throwing it up in the air. There's very little follow-through. The whole swing looks like a soft karate chop. Make sure your clubhead goes down under the ball.

With this shot, I find the ball lands deader on the green from a buried lie than any other way I've tried. It works well from soft sand or harder sand. You find the ball comes out with very little effort.

HILLY LIES

All the techniques I described in Chapter 9 apply to hilly lies in a bunker, with only a few exceptions.

On an uphill lie, you'll have to hit the ball much harder than on a flat lie.

This is because you're swinging through, parallel to the slope, sending the ball higher, but shorter. You can also play this shot with a short, crisp swing, hitting one inch behind the ball. It results in the ball flying lower with a lot of spin. A good shot to know.

On a downhill lie, play the ball back in the middle of your stance or even farther back depending on the severity of the lie. Make certain you open the blade enough to get the ball up. Swing down at a slightly steeper angle than the slope, going down with the knees. Enter the sand a little closer to the ball than usual.

When the ball is below your feet in a bunker, don't attempt to close the blade to prevent the ball flying to the right. Instead, use an open blade and aim more left of the flag than normal. On lies with the ball above your feet, compensate for the ball's tendency to fly to the left by aiming a little right of the flag.

LONG SHOTS

My maximum range with the sand wedge hitting one or two inches behind the ball is about thirty to forty yards. On shots longer than that, I go to a pitching wedge or a 9- or 8-iron. Because you need more distance, open your stance and blade only a little. Hit only one inch or so behind the ball, or closer if necessary. This is the hardest shot in golf. Through practice, I've made it my best shot!

The main thing on these longer shots is to have the guts to swing as hard as necessary to get the ball to the hole. On a forty-yard shot, for example, you have to hit the ball as hard as a driver.

FAIRWAY BUNKERS

If you have a poor lie, or if your ball is close to the lip of the bunker, never go for a miracle shot. Just take your medicine, and get the ball out on the fairway with your sand wedge. If your lie is good, then you can use a full shot.

Make sure you have good footing. If the sand is soft, grind your feet down enough to form a solid foundation. If you have to grind your feet down several inches, compensate by choking down on the club the same amount. Even if the sand is firm, choke down on the club a little for more control. Set up with your weight more on the insides of your feet, your knees slightly closer together than usual. This keeps you more stable. Also, stand a little taller to the ball to help you catch the ball cleanly. Use as little body movement as possible. It's mostly an arm and hand swing.

PRACTICE AND PRACTICE SWINGS

There's probably no shot in golf that can vary more than a sand shot. It can be anything from a soft half swing that sends the ball a few feet to a full swing, in which you swing as hard as you can. Therefore, once you've mastered the basic skid shot, practice from every conceivable distance. Also, don't just practice from good, level lies—try a buried lie one time, a hilly lie another, and so on. There are many kinds of sand: soft, hard-packed, coarse, fine.

Because every sand shot is individual, it's very important to take a couple of practice swings outside the bunker. As you do so, try to see in your mind the length and pace of the swing you're going to use, how the ball will fly in the air, the landing spot, the ball's spin and roll—everything. Then put the same move on the ball.

12

Putt the Way You Swing

Ben Hogan once said that putting is a different game from the rest of golf. The acceptance of this idea has obscured a very important fact about the game. Many of the top players putt in the same manner as they swing.

Whether you look at tempo, rhythm, pattern (method of setting up to the ball) or even the type of swing, the similarities are startling. Here are some examples of this phenomenon.

Bobby Locke. In his full swing, Locke aims many yards to the right of target, then in the downswing comes over the top and hooks the ball back on line. He does the same thing in his putting, aiming as much as six feet right on his long putts, then pull/hooking them back to the hole.

Gary Player. Player copied Locke. He aims right and hooks the ball in the long game, and aims right and comes over the top in his putting.

Lee Trevino. Trevino is at the opposite end of the spectrum from Locke and Player. He aims left and push/slices his long shots, and aims slightly left and pushes his putts into the hole.

Ben Crenshaw. Crenshaw has a long, flowing swing from a wide stance and tends to swing from open to closed. His putting is the same.

Arnold Palmer. In his full swing, Palmer closes the clubface going back, then hangs on tightly with his left hand in the downswing to keep the clubface open. When Arnie was holing everything in sight, his putting style also was from closed to open.

Bob Charles. One of the great putters of all time, Charles putts with an "arm-and-shoulder" style with very little wrist. His full swing is very similar: a stiffish, though rhythmical, action with firm wrists.

Jack Nicklaus. All of Nicklaus' movements and gestures are very similar on and off the green. There's the same deliberation, the same tempo, even the same slightly open stance. Both in putting and the full swing, Jack has a very slow backswing. There's even the same slight pause at the top of each swing.

128. You should putt the way you swing. Bobby Locke, in his full swing, aimed to right field and then came over the top and hooked the ball back to the target. 129. He did the same when putting, aiming as much as six feet right of the hole on his long putts, then pull/hooking them back to the hole.

The "putt the way you swing" principle means that, whatever type of swing you have, you should develop the same type of putting stroke. Don't try to force a stroke on the green that is not natural to you.

If you're a smooth swinger from tee to green, don't try to "pop" (jab) your putts. If you swing from closed to open in the long game, don't try to putt from open to closed, and vice versa. If you have a waltz-type rhythm in your full swing, don't try a piston-like "one-two" rhythm in putting. Before you know it, an unnatural move in your putting stroke can work its way into your full swing.

I think there's one major exception to all this: if you feel more comfortable putting left-handed and swinging right-handed, I give you my blessing.

I'm a left-handed person swinging with right-handed clubs. My dominant eye is my left eye. At this point in time, I feel that I probably would have been better off putting left-handed. This is because, with your dominant eye farther from the hole, you can see the line better. To find out which eye is your dominant eye, take a sheet of paper and cut a circular hole, about one inch in diameter, in the middle of it. Holding the sheet of paper at arm's length in front of you at eye level, look through the hole and frame a small object a few yards away—a light switch, for example—in the middle of the hole. Keep both eyes open as you are doing this.

Now close your right eye. If the light switch stays in the middle of the circle, then you're sighting with your left eye, and that is your dominant eye. To check, open your right eye, then close your left. The hole in the paper should jump to the left of the light switch.

If your right eye is dominant, then the light switch stays centered when you close your left eye and jumps right if you close your right eye.

What brought this to mind was a recent arrival on Tour: Mac O'Grady. Mac is left-handed but can actually play almost equally well from the left and right sides. On Tour, he swings right-handed, but he putts left-handed, because his left eye is his dominant eye.

I must admit that, like every rule, there are exceptions to it. Bob Charles, who is right-handed but plays and putts left-handed, told me that his dominant eye was his right.

Be that as it may, my main purpose was to tell you that switching from righty in the long game to lefty on the green is OK. If it works on the Tour, who is to say it's wrong? This may be the piece of information that will be important to a future champion.

THE ARM-AND-SHOULDER STROKE

My own putting style closely mirrors my long game. The main difference is that, as in my new chipping style, I gear everything to taking the putter pretty much straight back and through.

130–133. In my putting stroke, I use the reverse overlap grip, and put about 60 percent of my weight on my left foot. I use an "arm-and-shoulder" stroke, with very little wrist, on short putts. On longer putts, I do use some wrist. As in the full swing, I key on maintaining the angle in my left wrist.

My putting grip is the reverse overlap, in which my left index finger over-laps the last three fingers of my right hand. However, this is strictly a matter of preference. Bobby Locke, for example, used his regular overlap grip for both putting and the long game.

One thing that all good putters do is to have both thumbs straight down the top of the grip. This position gives you maximum feel.

My setup is almost identical to that in chipping. The major difference is that, in putting, I position the ball off my left heel so that I can roll the ball. In chipping, you rarely get as good a lie as in putting, so it's safer to chip with the ball in the middle of the stance.

I use a slightly open stance, my feet about twelve inches apart. I also put 60 percent of my weight on my left foot; this helps to prevent swaying. However, many good putters prefer having their weight about evenly distrib-uted between their feet. Keep your weight on the balls and heels of your feet, not on your toes.

I bend forward quite a lot from the waist over the ball, my derriere well back, my hands and arms and the club close to my body. This allows my arms and the club to swing back and through on a vertical plane, much like the pendulum of a grandfather clock. I position my head over the target line. My head is up. I'm looking at the ball over my cheekbones. This position allows a golfer to sight the line best.

The top of the grip is level with the ball. The hands are in the slightly arched position that I described in Chapter 2. This minimizes wristiness. If you feel more comfortable positioning the putter grip higher on the pad of your left hand to accommodate the arched position, that's fine, although you don't have to. To get the correct arch in your hands, stand erect, grip the putter and hold it in front of you at waist level. Now let the putter head drop as far as it can with you retaining your grip. That's the wrist position you want.

The Stroke

In the stroke, I use what is called an "arm-and-shoulder" stroke, with little wrist. On short putts, anything inside about twenty feet, I try to be as wristless as possible. On longer putts, I think it's natural to use a little wrist. The key to the "arm-and-shoulder" stroke is to putt with your forearms, and your shoulders will follow.

On a short putt, say a five-footer, in which the putter goes back about six inches and through about six inches, the putter pretty much follows the target line back and through, and the clubface remains square to the target line. On longer putts, the putter naturally swings back to the inside and through to the inside. The putter face appears to open slightly going back, and close in the follow-through.

I say "appears" because, in actuality, the clubface remains square to the

134. At address, I set up with a slightly open stance. I bend forward quite a lot, from the waist, over the ball, my derriere well back, my hands and arms and the club close to my body. I position my eyes over the target line. My hands are slightly arched to minimize wristiness.

shoulder line back and through, as in the full swing. However, because the toe of the putter does lead the heel through the ball, this puts a little hook spin on the ball. The result is a putt that rolls very well.

I would say that 90 percent of the players on the PGA Tour putt this way.

Some players have taken this hook spin action a stage further. Bobby Locke aims right of the hole and then comes "over the top" with a "pull/hook" action. Gary Player does the same. Of the younger players, Ben Crenshaw and John Cook also aim a little right and use an "open-to-closed" action.

Nothing rolls a ball better than a hook in the long game. The same is true in putting.

A small minority of pros, say 5–7 percent, putt a different way. They use an "arm-and-shoulder" stroke but take the putter straight back and through along the target line, the clubface remaining square to the target line. Most of these pros have worked with Dave Pelz, a club manufacturer who has done a lot of research into putting and the stroke. Most notable examples are Tom Kite and Jim Simons. The way they get the putter to swing this way is to position the hands directly beneath the shoulders—that's the key.

My problem with this method is that the overwhelming majority of Tour players follow the natural style I first described. Most youngsters, I've noticed too, find it natural to take the putter back inside on longer putts, and let the blade "open and close." That's why I find it difficult to recommend the Kite/Simons/Pelz style, which, technically speaking, is a "closed to open" style. If many more players on Tour used it, I'd feel different.

I must admit that, at one time, I used to putt shut to open. It was natural for me then to have my hands under my shoulders. However, I don't putt that way any more.

In the full swing, I emphasized the importance of maintaining the angle in the back of your left wrist. The same principle applies in putting. The angle created where the back of your left hand and wrist meet should remain as constant as possible during your stroke. As in the short game, if your left wrist breaks down, so that a bigger angle appears in the back of your left wrist, this increases the loft of the putter. Your putt will always finish short of the hole with this action, and many times left.

One reason why your left wrist can break down is concentrating too much on the clubhead. If you're thinking of your hands moving the clubhead back and through, it's very easy to get too wristy, with the clubhead swinging back and through and the putter handle doing nothing. However, if you concentrate on the forearms swinging the grip end of the putter, both ends of the club move back and through.

Another "clubhead problem" comes from trying to keep the clubhead low. In a good stroke, the clubhead does stay low, but this is a result of swinging correctly. Forcing it to stay low results in additional movements of the wrists and arms, which make the stroke less reliable.

Imagine a line running horizontally across the top of your grip at address. Then force the clubhead to stay low to the ground by pushing it down and away from the ball, and down and through to the hole. To do that, you have to straighten your left arm a little going back and your right arm going through. Your wrists have to bend to accommodate this action. If you study the handle end of the club, you'll see that the top of the grip dips well below the horizontal line on the backswing and follow-through.

For most ordinary golfers, it's impossible to be consistent, with the handle bobbing up and down like this. Arnold Palmer does it, but he's the exception that proves the rule.

With an arm-and-shoulder stroke, the top of the grip will describe a little arc, rising a little in the backswing and follow-through. However, *feeling* as though it stays level is a good key whether you use an arm-and-shoulder or a wristy stroke.

"Wristy?" you say. "I thought you were trying to get me to use as little wrist as possible!" Okay. Probably the easiest way to have a consistent stroke and keep the top of the grip on a semilevel plane is with the arm-and-shoulder style I've been talking about, but there is another way.

Billy Casper, a great wristy putter in his prime, and still successful as a senior, anchors the top of his grip by setting his left forearm solidly against the inside of his left thigh at address and keeping it there in the stroke. In this way the top of his grip never moves. Casper is using a pendulum swing, with his left wrist as its center. It's a smaller pendulum than the one used in the arm-and-shoulder method (with its center between the shoulders), but it's effective and it's lasted well in competition. So I, for one, won't say it's wrong. In fact, if you're naturally a wristy putter, then I think that's the method to use.

Casper's stroke also takes the putter back and through along the target line, with the clubface remaining square to the target line.

Phil Rodgers put the end of the handle into his belly to anchor it. He used an extra-long putter.

The reason I advocate the arm-and-shoulder stroke is that it's a simpler stroke than a wristy stroke. It has less moving parts and therefore less to go wrong. It's also the type of stroke used by practically all Tour players today.

WORKING ON YOUR STROKE

I'm a great believer in working on your stroke away from the course. If you have some carpet that roughly simulates the surface of the green, and a full-length mirror, you're in business. You can check your grip, stance, stroke, everything.

Here are additional self-checking tips I've found useful.

Eyes over the Line. Address the ball exactly as if you were going to putt. Then, keeping the body in the same position, take your putter and hold it at the top of the grip with the index finger and thumb of one hand. Let the putter head dangle down. Bring the butt of the putter up *slowly* until it touches your nose. By sighting down the club shaft, you can then see if your eyes are over the target line or not. It's also important for a line across your eyes to line up over the target line. With your eyes askew, you get a distorted picture of the line to the hole, and misaim the putt. Ask a buddy to check you on this.

Putt a Penny. The bottom of your stroke should be right at the ball. In other words, when your putter contacts the ball, it should be traveling horizontally to the ground. If you hit down on the ball, it will pop up in the air before starting to roll. It will do the same thing if you hit up on it. If you can make a sixty-foot putt without the ball "hopping," you have a good stroke.

Your first warning on this problem is usually on long putts, in which you're hitting the ball harder.

I had the "pop-up" problem in college one time, and the way I cured it was

135–137. Billy Casper, one of the greatest wristy putters ever, anchors the top end of the grip by setting his left forearm solidly against his left thigh. He uses a pendulum swing with the left wrist as its center. It's a smaller pendulum than the one used in the arm-shoulder stroke, but it's very effective.

to put a penny down on a linoleum floor of our dormitory and try to putt a penny along the floor. At first, I couldn't even hit the penny, because I was hitting up on the ball so badly. When I started contacting the penny consistently, and it slid across the floor, my stroke straightened out in a hurry, and the ball rolled true again out on the course.

You can tell which problem you have—"hit up" or "hit down"—by how the penny reacts. If you're hitting "up," you miss the coin entirely, as I did initially. If the coin jumps up and skitters forward with a wobbling action, you're hitting down.

To correct the problem, start with address. Is the ball too far forward in your stance ("hit up") or back ("hit down")? Do you have too much weight on your left foot ("hit down") or your right foot ("hit up")? If these check out okay, then look for a sway in the swing, or excess wristiness.

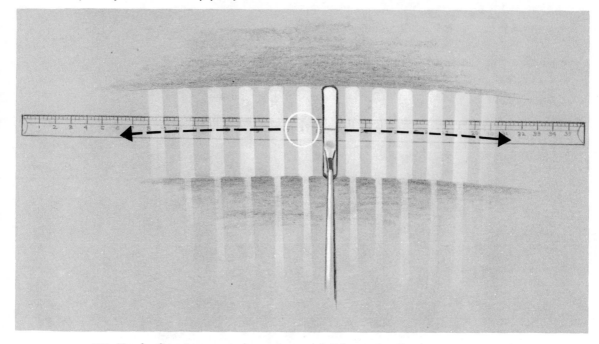

138. To check out your stroke, put a yardstick on the floor as your target line and address an imaginary ball in the center of the yardstick. If you're using an arm-shoulder stroke, you can see if the putter goes straight back and through on a six-inch stroke, and on longer strokes from slightly inside to slightly inside. You can also see the blade opening and closing by referring to the inch marks on the yardstick.

Straight Back, Straight Through. To check out your stroke, put a yardstick on the floor as your target line and address an imaginary ball in the middle of the yardstick. Now swing.

If you're using the "natural" arm-and-shoulder stroke I recommended, you can readily see if the putter goes straight back and through on a six-inch stroke, and on longer strokes from slightly inside to slightly inside. You can also see the blade "opening and closing" by referring to the inch marks on the yardstick.

If you're using one of the "straight back, straight through" strokes, you can also check your swing path and clubface against the yardstick.

Sweet-Spot Hit. Every putter has a sweet spot on the clubface. If you strike the ball on the sweet spot, the putter head stays square to the line of swing through impact. You get the full force out of your stroke. However, if you strike the ball to the toe side of the sweet spot, the clubface is kicked open, and the ball is hit weakly and finishes short and to the right of target. If you strike the ball to the heel side of the sweet spot, the clubface is kicked closed, and the ball finishes short and to the left. The more you hit on the toe or heel, the worse you putt.

To find the sweet spot on your putter, hold the shaft just below the grip with your right hand. Bring your right hand up in front of you, a little above your head, so that the sole of the putter is horizontal and the clubface faces you. Hold the shaft of the putter as lightly as you can while still keeping the putter in this position. Now take a pencil in your left hand and tap the pencil along the clubface from toe to heel. You'll be able to feel the toe kicking back when you tap the toe, and the heel kicking back on a heel tap. When you've found the sweet spot, where the clubhead is knocked straight back with no rotation, mark it on the top of your putter.

Some manufacturers identify the sweet spot on a putter with a line on the top of the head. The problem with that is that sometimes the line is in the wrong place or there's simply no line at all.

FIND AND KEEP YOUR TEMPO

Every teacher agrees that a decelerating stroke—one in which you swing back at one speed and slow down through the ball—is no good. It's just too variable. You slow down more one time, less another time—it becomes impossible to judge distance.

The same teachers still recommend an accelerating stroke. Why, I can't understand. The same arguments that destroy the decelerating stroke apply equally well to the accelerating stroke. You speed up through the ball more one time, less another time, and don't know how far the ball is going to roll. Constantly thinking of speeding up the downswing can lead to a really jerky stroke.

I think you should swing back and through with one speed, *your* speed. The tempo you use should match the tempo on your full swing. As I said earlier, if you use a fast tempo in your full swing, use a fast tempo in your putting. If your full swing is slow and deliberate, your putting stroke should be slow and deliberate.

To help maintain a constant tempo, think of keeping the same miles per hour back and through. If I swing back at 5 mph, I swing through at 5 and not 3 or 10.

Another trick is to swing to a cadence. I make a couple of practice strokes, saying to myself, "One-two, one-two." "One" is for the backswing, "two" for the downswing. Then I putt the ball with the same one-two action. If you have a slower tempo than mine, try a "one-and-two" cadence.

Sometimes you can be under such pressure that even a cadence is not enough. When you're coming down to the wire in a tournament, the mind starts to race. You start walking faster, and your tempo speeds up.

I had such an experience when I won the Sun City in southern Africa in '82. It was the first hole of the playoff, and Seve Ballesteros had almost knocked his ball in the hole for a gimme two. I had a seven-footer downhill with a six-inch break. Now, the first prize was $500,000, second $160,000—a $340,000 difference. So, believe me, I was nervous. I decided that, just before I stroked the ball, I'd close my eyes and make a nice, even-tempo putt. I did, knocking the ball right in the heart of the hole. I used this same technique a couple of other times in the playoff and, in the end, it won the tournament for me.

I don't guarantee that you'll hole every pressure putt by closing your eyes, but at least you'll make a decent run at it. You won't have the putter "exploding" through the ball.

READING AND BELIEVING

To be a good putter, it's not enough to merely have a good stroke. You've got to be able to "read" greens. This means being able to see all the conditions that affect a putt so that you know how hard to hit the ball and on what line to start the ball.

There are basically three elements that affect a putt. They are slope, grain and the pace of the green.

Slope. You've probably seen pros get down behind the ball on the green and look toward the hole. What they're doing is reading the "break," the amount, if any, the ground slopes to the right or left. If the ground slopes to the right, you have to allow for the break by aiming to the left of the hole, and vice versa.

The other part of "slope" is whether you're putting uphill toward the hole or downhill. If you're putting uphill, you have to strike the putt harder, and the less you allow for any break factor. If you're putting downhill, you have to strike the ball more softly and allow for more break than on a level putt.

Grain. Grain is the direction in which the grass is growing. If you're putting in the same direction the grass is growing, or "downgrain," the ball will roll faster than usual, and you have to hit the ball a little softer than usual. If you're putting "upgrain," against the direction the grass is growing, the putt will be slower, and you have to hit the ball harder. If, as you look from ball to hole, the grass is growing to the right across your line to the hole, the grain causes the ball to roll to the right, and you must allow for this by starting the ball to the left of the hole. If the grass is growing to the left, start the ball to the right of the hole. On these "cross-grain" putts, the grain acts in much the same way as slope to the left or right.

Grain is more a factor in Bermuda grass, a wiry strain used mostly in the South. The effect is less in bent grass, used in the Midwest and the North. Bermuda grass follows the setting sun. Thus, grain on most flat greens is dominantly lying west to southwest. Play for it if it's there.

When reading grain, simply get down close enough to see which way the grass is growing. Look for light or dark patches of grass. If the grass is light and shiny as you look at it, then the grass is growing or leaning away from you. If it's dark, then the grass is growing toward you.

One of the best ways that I've come up with to read both break and grain is to imagine that I have poured a bucket of water on the green. Then I picture which way the water would run. Both break and grain tend to go with the contour of the green, the way the water would run off the green.

When you're playing a strange course, always ask the club pro if there are any peculiarities about the greens. He may say things like "They break toward the creek" or "away from the mountain." It's invaluable information.

It's also worth noting that grain affects hitting irons into a green. If the ball lands into the grain, it will pop up and go nowhere; if downgrain, it takes a long, skidding bounce.

Pace. Two elements affect the pace of the green. The lower the grass is cut the faster the ball will roll over it and the more gently you must strike the ball. If the grass is relatively high, the green is "slower," and you have to strike the ball harder. A dry green is also faster than a wet green.

Although most people only talk of slope, grain and pace, in reality there is a fourth factor, and that's wind. A light wind obviously won't affect the roll of a putt much. However, if you ever play in a big wind, take the direction of the wind into your calculations before you putt.

As in chipping, if you switch from a Surlyn ball to a balata, or vice versa, you must hit enough practice putts with the ball you're going to use so that you adjust your touch to the new ball.

Once you have taken all the factors into account on a putt, you have a clear mental picture of how the ball will roll toward the hole. It's like going to the movies. You see yourself making the stroke, the ball starting, say, to the left, taking the break and then dropping into the hole. Then you go ahead and execute the putt.

A good putter is one who programs and visualizes success. He always sees the ball going into the hole. If he misses a putt, he simply analyzes why he missed it, and then doesn't dwell on it. He knows that not all putts will go in. He's patient.

A bad putter does the opposite. He remembers every putt he has missed. He tells himself he's a bad putter. He programs and visualizes missing putts —and does.

If you want to be a good putter, you must believe that you are a good putter. If you have a bad day on the greens, tell yourself that this is nothing like what you normally do. Say to yourself, "I'm a good putter," and that's what you'll be.

139. A good putter programs and visualizes success. He always sees the putt going into the hole.

13

Playing the Game

Most of this book has been concerned with developing a good swing, and with the various shots you need from tee through green. Now I want to look at the big picture: how you should play the game. It's as though we've just built a car together. Now we're going to go and drive it.

PLOT YOUR COURSE

Before I play a round, I develop a game plan for that course. In other words, I go through the course hole by hole and decide where I'm going to place each shot and with what club. You also should develop such a plan for your home course. Make the plan as practical as possible. Take into account your game's strengths and weaknesses.

A vital part of any game plan is what we pros call the "yardages." These are the key distances you need to know coming into the greens.

On par 4 holes, you need to pace off the yardage from your usual landing area, using a convenient object such as a tree or a sprinkler head, to the front, middle and back of the green. Then you're prepared for any pin position. On par 5's, pace off the yardage from where your second shot usually lands. Usually, on par 3's all you need to pace off is the distance from the front of the green to the middle and from the middle to the back. This is because you can use the permanent yardage markers on the tee, which give the distance from the marker to the center of the green. If your course doesn't have permanent markers, then pace off the yardage from the back of the tee to the front, middle and back of the green.

If you followed my earlier advice on finding out the distance you hit with each club, you're ready to start.

In selecting a target area for your tee shot on a par 4 or par 5, what you have to find is the spot from which you'd most like to play your second shot —generally the one that lets you hit into the opening of the green. You must always think one shot ahead.

If there are mounds on the left side of the fairway and a flatter area to the right, then you may want to aim for the right side of the fairway. Sometimes you have little choice: the whole fairway slopes to the left or right. In this case you must aim to land the ball on the high side of the slope so that it rolls down into the middle of the fairway.

The length you want to hit a tee shot can also be critical. Say there are fairway bunkers in the landing area. If you can lay up short of them and still hit a club for your second shot that easily gets you on the green, then going to a 3- or a 4-wood may be a smart play. If laying up would leave you a second shot with a wood or a long iron, and the green is small, then you should probably try to carry the bunkers and have a shorter iron into the green. Sometimes, using a driver from the tee can take you too far, say onto a downhill lie. If a slightly shorter tee shot would leave you on a flat spot, then take a fairway wood. On such holes, pace off the distance from tee to landing area.

There are two schools of thought when you have severe trouble to one side or the other of the hole. By severe trouble, I mean out of bounds (O.B.) or a water hazard, where you have to take a penalty shot. The first school says to start the ball at the trouble and work the ball away from it. The second says to start the ball away from the trouble and work it back. I subscribe to the second school.

Let's say you come to a tee with O.B. on the right and try to hit the ball at the O.B. and draw it back to the fairway. There are four possibilities, two of them of putting you into trouble:

1. the shot comes off as planned, 2. you hook the ball too much, 3. you hit the ball straight (O.B.) and 4. you slice the ball (O.B.).

If you go with my thinking and start the shot well to the left of the O.B. and fade it back, the possibilities are as follows:

1. the shot comes off as planned, 2. you hit the ball straight, 3. you hook the ball and 4. you overdo the fade and slice the ball O.B.

With the first school, two out of four possibilities go O.B., but with the second, my school, only one of four finds trouble.

When you want to fade or draw a ball from the tee, remember the techniques I mentioned in the shot-making chapter. For example, teeing the ball a little higher helps you draw the ball. Teeing it a little lower aids a fade. Remember, too, that the teeing ground is two club lengths deep. It may pay you to go back from the markers if you can find a lie that induces a fade (ball below feet) or a draw (ball above feet).

On par 3 holes, it is often a good idea to go back a little from the markers. If you tee up between the markers, you probably have to contend with a lot of divots. If you can find a divot mark that points straight at your target, you might like to tee the ball right behind it; you have a clear perspective of the line even when you're addressing the ball. Harry Vardon, who won the U.S. Open in 1900, and the British Open six times, was known for doing this, so it's a pretty good tip.

A lot of people will tell you that it's a good idea to draw the ball around the corner of a dogleg to the left and fade on a dogleg to the right. I disagree, unless you can play the shot consistently. A straight shot is a better percentage shot.

When you try to draw the ball around a dogleg to the left, you have a tendency to aim too close to the corner. The draw you played for comes off, but you're in the woods. You can also overdo the draw (hook) and go deep in the woods. If you play for a straight ball down the middle and you accidentally draw the ball, you probably will go around the corner of the dogleg in good shape. If you hit it straight or even slice the ball a little, you're all right too.

APPROACH SHOTS

On shots into the green, here are the factors you have to consider: your lie, stance and yardage, and the conditions up at the green. To evaluate these factors, I use a "stoplight" system that you can easily adapt to your game.

"Green Light" Situation. If there's nothing to keep you from firing directly at the flag, that's a "green light" situation. Your ball, let's say, is 165 yards away from the hole. The pin is at the back left of a long green. Bunkers guard the front left and the right side of the green. There are no bunkers at the back. Let's assume your normal distance with a 6-iron is 160 yards, so you're looking at a draw with a 6-iron to pick up the extra five yards. You check your lie and the ball is sitting up nicely. You realize that the bunker on the left should not come into play, because you're going to be landing the ball in the middle of the green. You've got yourself a green light.

"Yellow Light" Situation. If there are a couple of factors against you, then it's probably a "yellow light" situation, and you should play for the middle of the green. Let's assume the same circumstances as before except that now you have a very tight lie, the green is very shallow, and there's a bunker at the back of the green. You know that a tight lie favors a fade, not a draw. This, plus the tight pin placement, gives you a "yellow light," and you play safely to the center of the green.

"Red Light" Situation. When all the factors are against you, that gives you a "red light." The only thing to do is chip out. Let's assume the same length of shot, only now you're in the heavy rough to the right of the fairway. Your ball lies under trees, and to make it interesting, you have to carry a lake to

reach the green. A deep bunker guards the whole left side of the green. Even if you could hit the ball out with a medium iron, you wouldn't be able to carry the lake. If you try to go for the opening, you won't be able to stop the ball and it probably will go into the bunker on the left. All you can do is punch the ball out short of the green in the best position to chip and putt for your par.

In adapting the stoplight system to your game, you have to realize that one person's green light can be another's yellow. If the shot calls for a draw, the lie is good and the draw is your favorite shot, that's green. If you can't hit a draw to save your life, then it's yellow.

How you're playing also affects how you apply the system. If you're playing well, you're probably going to have a lot of "green lights" that day. If you're playing badly, you may have to stick to yellow for the whole round.

You can feel free to apply the principles behind the stoplight system to playing par 3's. The only difference, of course, is that on a par 3, you always have a good lie.

BAD CONDITIONS

Although no one enjoys playing in the wind and wet, the main thing to realize is that the conditions are the same for everyone. The best way to approach bad weather is to think of it as a challenge to your shot-making skills. Beating it then becomes fun.

In the Wind

I guess that all golfers would admit that a drive with a following wind is one of their favorite shots. Yet, even with this comparatively easy shot, there are a couple of areas where you can go astray. Number one is trying for too much distance: swinging far too hard and mishitting the drive completely. Instead, just concentrate on putting a good, solid swing on the ball. Then you get the extra distance the wind can give you. If the wind is very strong, say over 20 mph, then a 3-wood sometimes will give you more distance than a driver.

When hitting into a green downwind, you have to take less club than usual. Don't try to help the ball up into the air. Just hit the ball flush with a normal flight. Occasionally, you may have to hit the ball high to clear a bunker. When you do, you'll have problems controlling distance.

Playing into the wind gives most golfers fits. Typically the ball gets up too high and falls short of target. If this happens to you, realize that you could be swinging too hard. A hard swing puts a lot of backspin on the ball.

You're much better off swinging a little more slowly than usual. This puts less backspin on the ball, and it bores through the wind. On approach shots, compensate for the slow swing and the wind by using a less lofted club than usual.

In a crosswind, the best strategy for maximum distance off the tee is to let the ball ride the wind. In a left-to-right wind, set up to the left of your target and slightly fade the ball. Aim right and draw the ball in a right-to-left wind.

If you need pinpoint accuracy on a tee shot, then aim straight at your target and put enough hook or slice on the ball to hold it straight. You'll lose a little distance, but it will be worth the sacrifice.

Hitting toward the pin, you again need accuracy. So hold the ball up into the wind with the right amount of hook or slice to keep it headed straight for the flag. The ball will drop softly on the green, because the sidespin fights the crosswind. If you use this technique, remember to take a stronger club than usual.

If you haven't reached the stage where you can deliberately hook or slice the ball, then, in a right-to-left wind, start the ball sufficiently to the right so that the wind brings the ball back to the target. Do the reverse in a left-to-right wind.

The above statements assume that you're using a balata ball. However, if you're using a Surlyn ball, it's great in a wind. It flies higher than a balata ball but bores through a headwind almost unaffected. In crosswinds, you only have to aim off very slightly. I won the British Open with a Surlyn-wound ball in 1976. I used it because of the wind and because the greens at Birkdale were so hard that no one could stop the ball on the greens.

In the Wet

In wet weather, damp and deep rough is extremely tough. You probably will lose a shot just about every time from such rough unless you know what to do: aim for the middle of the fairway and hit the ball solidly.

Don't try anything fancy—such as draws and fades—on a wet day. The shots won't work as easily, due to water getting between the clubface and the ball. You're also going to find that your long irons are very difficult to hit. Instead, use a 5-wood; it will get the ball up in the air much more easily.

In most cases, you need to take one club less than in dry conditions. This is because the ball shoots off a wet clubface, rather like in the "flier" lie. If the rain is falling as you play a shot, then the raindrops themselves resist the ball's flight and you probably need your normal club for the distance.

In the short game, don't try to chip with low-lofted clubs; you'll find it impossible to predict how the ball will roll. Instead, take more loft and fly the ball just short of the hole. It will skip once and stop. In putting, remember what I said about a wet green: hit the ball harder and play less break. You might even want to chip the ball when on the green if it's very wet.

PLAY THE PERCENTAGES

If you were to ask me the one reason most pros score well and most amateurs don't, excluding ball-striking ability, I would have to say, simply, that pros play the percentages.

Just about every situation in golf involves choosing between one shot and another. An amateur never says to himself, "Well, I can make this shot only one time out of ten, and the other shot I can make nine times out of ten." He just remembers the one time he made the first shot successfully. He plays a lot of "low percentage" shots, and misses most of them.

The pro always evaluates situations using the percentage method. The only time he picks a low-percentage shot is if it's forced on him by circumstances: he has to make that shot to win a tournament. Ninety-nine times out of a hundred, the pro picks the "high percentage" shot. It's smart golf.

To help you learn percentages, there's nothing better than the game Ben Hogan used to play called "worst ball": Hit two drives off the first tee—one finishes in the fairway, the other in the rough. Pick up the fairway ball, and play the one in the rough. Hit two second shots—one finishes on the green, the other in a greenside bunker. Pick up the ball on the green and play two balls from the bunker—one finishes three feet away, the other ten feet. Putt two balls from the ten-foot distance—and so on.

Besides learning percentages, the game makes you extremely tough mentally. You're having such "bad luck" all the time, it makes you concentrate twice as hard just to survive.

If you can break 80 playing "worst ball," you're ready for the Tour.

14

Program Your Mind

Although a sound swing and all-round shot-making ability count for a lot in golf, the difference between winners and losers is their mental attitude.

A winner programs himself for success in much the same way a computer operator uses the right software for a certain function. A loser programs failure.

To program your mental computer, use a process called visualization. This means "seeing" something in your mind or forming a mental picture of it. Before you do anything in life, you have to form the right mental picture.

Suppose your teacher gives you an assignment to talk to the class about your hobby, photography. If you're wise, you prepare your talk by jotting down the topics you want to cover: types of camera, film, picture-taking techniques, composition and so on. As you do so, you see yourself talking about these things to the class. After a while, you form mental pictures of presenting topics in one order or another. You then pick the best order. When you give your speech, you find yourself using the exact same words and order you visualized beforehand. You may take a list of topics with you to class, but if you've done a good job on visualizing the speech, you often find you barely glance at the list.

Suppose you hadn't bothered to prepare in any way. You wouldn't have formed any mental picture of your speech. As a result, it would be a mess—a mere jumble of ideas.

Now let's suppose your one and only reaction to the assignment was to say to yourself, "I can't do it. I'm too scared to give a speech." I'll guarantee you, you won't be able to get up out of your chair.

Now, I'm not saying that visualization will stop your being nervous. It won't. But do a good job on visualization, and you'll perform despite your nerves.

I hope I've made one point perfectly clear. You get out of your mental computer what you put into it. Computer people have a saying, "GIGO." That stands for "Garbage in, garbage out." What I want you to do is forget the "garbage"—negative thoughts. Put good, positive pictures into your mind, and you'll get the results you want. This applies whether you're working on your swing, individual shots or your goals.

PROGRAM YOUR SWING

As a beginner, you obviously have no mental picture of how to make the proper golf swing. What you must do is emulate the best model swings you can find. I've given you several to study in this book. However, that should just be a beginning.

You should take every opportunity to gather good mental pictures of the swing. Study sequence photos in magazines and books. Watch the slow-motion swings of the top pros shown on TV, and maybe tape them for study. Come to a PGA Tour event and look at the pros in person.

One of the fun things to do at a tournament is to position yourself down one end of the practice ground so that you can see up to twenty players in a row. Let your eyes go down the line. See if you can pick out the top players just by the quality of their swings. Compare what they do that the lesser players don't.

Eventually, you develop a list of points that make your swing work best. These "swing keys" trigger the right moves for you.

Mental pictures are the way to program your mind and, through it, your swing. However, the "Sam Snead / Sam Shank" principle still applies. Have photos taken of your swing, whether they're still pictures, movies or videos. Use your full-length mirror. Only if what you think you're doing and what you're actually doing are the same do you have any chance to improve.

PROGRAM YOUR SHOTS

Earlier in this book I gave a preshot pattern or routine, a list of physical steps you make before a shot. The pattern takes care of such mechanics as taking the grip, spreading the feet, positioning the ball, and so on. However, it also keeps your mind on the positive things you want to do; it prevents any "GIGO." It gives you the time to form the right mental pictures.

As you come to the ball, immediately start forming mental pictures of possible shots. Start with your lie, then study the yardage, the conditions and the situation in the target area. It's important, I think, to "play" these alternative shots in your mind in their entirety: see the swing you'd use, the flight of the ball and its roll, the complete result. The more vivid the "movie" you run through your head on each shot, the better able you are to make the right choice.

Once you've decided what shot to hit, visualize again the swing and the ball's flight, its roll and where it finishes. Then go and hit the ball.

I do most of this "movie-making" when I'm standing behind the ball looking down toward the target. I generally run through the swing one more time in my mind as I settle into my stance.

To help you visualize the final swing you want to make, remember you can use anything that will help you form a clearer mental picture. You can use a swing key, such as "Drive the handle through the ball." You can imagine you're Gary Player because you need a "hook" swing. If you have a particularly tough shot, I've found it useful to remember the best shot of this type I've ever played. Whatever works for you, use it.

PROGRAM YOUR EMOTIONS

Once you get into competition, you're going to find that one of the most difficult things to control is your emotional level. At times, you're so nervous, you feel you're about to explode. At others, you're dragging along; you're so "low," it's tough to keep interested.

I think emotions are like the tachometer of a car. At 6,000 revolutions per minute, your engine is revving so hard, it blows up. About 5,800 RPM is probably your most efficient level, where you can play best without blowing up.

If you're in contention in a tournament, really under pressure, you have to know how to cope, how to lower your revs just a mite so you avoid going over that red line.

I have several tricks that I use that will help. One thing I do is to downplay everything. I'll say to myself, "Hey, the worst you can do is lousy" or "Just do the best you can—if it works, fine." It may sound negative, but you have to use something to lower the tension. Or think how beautiful the day is, how lucky you are or how nice the course is.

Another method I use is to think of past successes. I'll say, "Hey, you played well in the stretch at L.A. You can do it again." Granted, you may not have the successes I have to recall. As you get more experience, recall *any* success you've had to program success here and now. If you were able to hang tough in the club championship last year, use that, if necessary, to help you in this year's state amateur.

I had to play these types of games at Sun City in '82. I was walking down the 18th fairway and was getting very nervous. I knew it. So I said to myself, "Hey, this isn't really playing for half a million bucks. This is for making the cut for the Tucson Open [the next event on the PGA Tour]. I can handle that." I convinced myself, and hit a great shot into the green, then almost made the putt.

Sometimes, of course, you're playing badly and you're not too enthusiastic. What do you do then? This may sound funny, but I'll have my caddie say to me, "I'll bet you a buck that you can't play three under par from here on in." I'll say, "Oh yeah!" It's a funny thing, but I become more motivated by that buck than all the thousands I may be playing for.

PROGRAM YOUR GOALS

If you want to improve, you've got to believe in yourself. You've also got to believe that you are improving and do everything you can to improve.

Gary Player is a shining example of what I mean. The man is over fifty years old, yet he never lives in the past. He's always telling you how well he is hitting the ball now, not twenty years ago.

He's also not afraid to change. A few years back, Gary used to have a pronounced "reverse C" in his follow-through. His back was hurting with this action. Now Gary "walks through" on just about every full shot. He knows he can't hurt his back with that action. He *is* hitting the ball better than ever.

The way to reach your goal in golf, whether that's to be a Tour player or a good amateur, is to set your final goal and then mentally picture all the different rungs up the ladder to that goal.

In your case, this might be winning your club's junior championship, then maybe the city or state junior, then the National Junior. Whatever the rungs are, they're important, because they give you something to shoot at on your way to your final goal.

They're also a way of making sure that you never lack motivation. If you win a tournament, no matter what tournament, it's easy to get complacent, and your game suffers. If you always have another goal in front of you, you stay sharp.

15

A Code of Honor

Although it's outside the scope of this book to tell you all about the *Rules of Golf,* I would be delinquent if I didn't talk about them at all. I think it's up to every golfer, including juniors, to learn the Rules and play by them. If you don't, then you may be playing a game involving a golf club and a ball, but it's not golf.

YOU'RE THE JUDGE

Golf is unique among games because so often you are the judge as to whether you've broken a rule or not. The Rules put you on your honor to call a violation on yourself.

I was playing in a college event called the Beehive Invitational. I was leading the tournament and came to this par 3, where I hit my ball into a long rut just short of the green, I went up to the ball, knocked it stiff, and tapped it into the hole. When I picked the ball out of the hole, I saw that it was the wrong ball—it wasn't my ball. Now, nobody knew it was the wrong ball but me. It would have been very, very easy for me to just go ahead and say nothing.

I told the guys I was playing with what had happened, and we went back and found my ball. I ended up taking a two-stroke penalty and played out the hole with my own ball. The story did have a happy ending, though. I did win the tournament.

SOME BASICS

If you knew just two rules, you actually would be a pretty honest golfer, *Rule 1* says, "The Game of Golf consists in playing a ball from the teeing ground into a hole by a stroke or successive strokes in accordance with the Rules." *Rule 13-1* says, "The ball shall be played as it lies, except as otherwise provided in the Rules."

A lot is implied in these two simple rules. You play "a ball," not several. You can't start off the hole with one ball and play someone else's ball into the hole, as I accidentally did in the Beehive. You advance the ball with strokes made with a club, not by pushes or a foot mashie. You play the ball "as it lies." This means that, basically, you must accept the lie that results from any stroke. You can't nudge the ball into a better spot.

Of course, there are circumstances when your ball ends in places where the Rules have to help you put it (or another ball) back in play. That's why Rule 13-1 has to include that phrase at the end. The most common are as follows:

Man-made Objects. You get relief without penalty from any man-made objects on the course outside of water hazards. Say your ball finishes under a bench. If you can move the bench, do that and then play your ball. If your ball comes to rest on a sprinkler head, you obviously can't move it. Then the Rules allow you to drop the ball within one club length of the nearest spot where the sprinkler head no longer interferes with your stance or swing, but not nearer the hole.

Unfair Conditions. The Rules consider that you shouldn't be expected to play from some natural conditions. The first is "casual water," a temporary accumulation of water such as a puddle after a thunderstorm. The second is "Ground Under Repair," often called G.U.R., which basically is ground on which the golf course crew is working. The third is a hole made by a burrowing animal, reptile or bird. In all three cases, the Rules allow you to drop the ball within one club length of the nearest spot where the condition no longer interferes with your stance or swing, not nearer the hole. No penalty.

Out of Bounds. If your ball finishes outside white stakes anywhere on the course, then you're out of bounds (or O.B.). You have to go back to the place from which you played the ball, and play another ball. Count both strokes and add a one-stroke penalty to your score for the hole.

Water Hazards. If your ball goes into a water hazard (any sea, lake, pond, river, ditch or anything similar) and you can't play it, you have two options: You can either use the same procedure as for O.B. or you can drop another ball behind the hazard. Keep the point where the ball last crossed the hazard margin between yourself and the hole. You can drop back as far as you like along that imaginary line. You add one penalty stroke to your score for the hole.

Some water hazards are what is known as "lateral." Your course's scorecard will tell you which hazards are lateral. If your ball goes in a lateral water hazard, you can drop another ball, under one stroke penalty, within two club lengths of the point where the ball last crossed the hazard margin, not nearer the hole, or a point on the opposite side of the hazard the same distance from the hole. You also have the choice of proceeding under either of the water-hazard options.

Unplayable Ball. If your ball lands in such a bad place, in a cleft of rock for example, that you can't play it, the Rules allow you to move it, but under penalty. You have three options—choose the one that gives you the best relief: You can use the same procedure as for O.B. Your other options are to drop a ball, under one stroke penalty, either within two club lengths of the spot where the ball lay, but not nearer the hole, or behind the spot where the ball lay, keeping the spot directly between yourself and the hole. Again, there's no limit to how far behind the spot you can drop the ball.

Although I've condensed some of the more common Rules here, I must point out that even what I've just given you is far from complete. Every beginning golfer should obtain the complete *Rules of Golf* booklet and keep it in his or her bag. To obtain a copy of the booklet, send $1.00 to: USGA, Golf House, Far Hills, N.J. 07931.

The Rules booklet has recently been completely reorganized and is a far handier book than in the past. When I was growing up, you had to burrow around in the Index to the Rules to find the rule you wanted. Even then, you constantly got lost. In this new edition, the Table of Contents steers you easily to the rule you're looking for. There's really no excuse for not playing by the Rules.

I think you know me well enough by now to realize that the reason why you should play by the Rules is because it's the right thing to do.

One last point. You can hardly expect your game to improve, and you feel better about it, if you're a cheat. If you want your prayers to be answered and to become a great golfer, I would highly recommend that you play golf fair, square and by the Rules.

JOHNNY MILLER

Career Victories

1964   U.S. Junior championship
1971   *Southern Open
1972   *Heritage Classic
       Otago Classic (New Zealand)
1973   *U.S. Open championship
       World Cup (Spain), individual and team championship (with Jack Nicklaus)
       Lancôme Trophy (France)

* Indicates PGA Tour victories

1974   *Bing Crosby National Pro-Am
      *Phoenix Open
      *Tucson Open
      *Heritage Classic
      *Tournament of Champions
      *Westchester Classic
      *World Open
      *Kaiser International
      Dunlop Phoenix championship (Japan)

1975   *Phoenix Open
      *Tucson Open
      *Bob Hope Desert Classic
      *Kaiser International
      World Cup (Thailand), individual and team championship (with Lou Graham)

1976   *Tucson Open
      *Bob Hope Desert Classic
      British Open championship

1979   Lancôme Trophy (France)

1980   *Inverrary Classic

1981   *Tucson Open
      *Los Angeles Open

1982   *San Diego Open
      Sun City Million-Dollar Challenge, Republic of Bophuthatswana, in southern Africa

1983   *Inverrary Classic
      *Chrysler Team Invitational (with Jack Nicklaus)

1984   Spalding Invitational

Some Career Highlights

Johnny Miller was born April 29, 1947, in San Francisco, California. At age seventeen he won the U.S. Junior. At nineteen he signed up to caddie in the 1966 U.S. Open at the Olympic Club, in San Francisco, but then qualified for the championship and finished eighth. He went to Brigham Young University, where he was 1st Team All-American. In 1969 he qualified for the PGA Tour. In the 1973 U.S. Open, he came from six strokes off the pace to score 63 in the final round and win. In 1974, Miller won the first three events on the PGA Tour schedule, finishing the year with eight PGA Tour victories. He also set what was then a record for money won on Tour in a single year: $353,021. Since then, no one has won as many Tour events in a single year—the closest was Tom Watson's six victories in 1980. In 1975, Miller won the

* Indicates PGA Tour victories

Phoenix Open with a 24-under-par score; his winning margin was fourteen strokes. The following week, he won at Tucson with a 25-under-par score; his margin of victory was nine strokes. In each event he had a round of 61. He was a member of the 1975 U.S. Ryder Cup Team. His career earnings reached a million dollars on PGA Tour on February 8, 1976, with his win at the Bob Hope Desert Classic. The years 1977–79 were difficult for Miller, as he endured the worst, and most publicized, slump by a modern-day champion. In 1979, his comeback was foreshadowed by his close play-off loss to Tom Watson at the Hall of Fame Classic in August—Miller had shot a 63 en route to the tie. In October he won again in France at the Lancôme. In December he won the first Johnny Miller Invitational Pro-Am. He returned to the winner's circle on the PGA Tour in 1980 with his victory in the Inverrary Classic. He was a member of the 1981 U.S. Ryder Cup Team. In 1982, Miller won the biggest first prize in golf history ($500,000) in the Sun City Million-Dollar Challenge, beating Seve Ballesteros in a 9-hole play-off. He reached his second million dollars on the PGA Tour on April 1, 1984.

Desmond Tolhurst, Contributing editor to *Golf Magazine,* is a prolific writer who has collaborated with leading players and teachers on hundreds of instructional articles over the past twenty years. He has also coauthored several instructional books. Tolhurst lives in Bronxville, New York with his wife, Patricia, and two children.